A JOURNEY OF RICHES

IN SEARCH OF HAPPINESS

**Thirteen Voyages that will
Touch your Soul**

A Journey Of Riches - In Search of Happiness
Thirteen Voyages that will touch your Soul © 2019

Published by Motion Media International
Editing: Gwendolyn Parker, Chris Drabenstott and Donna Barclay
Cover Design: Motion Media International
Typesetting & Assembly: Motion Media International
Printing: Amazon and IngramSparks

Creator: John Spender - Primary Author
Title: *A Journey Of Riches - In Search of Happiness*
ISBN Digital: 978-1-925919-01-1
ISBN Print: 978-1-925919-02-8
Subjects: Self-Help, Motivation/Inspiration and Spirituality.

Artist: Ritu Bali

❖ Acknowledgments

Reading and writing is a gift that too few give to themselves. It is such a powerful way to reflect and gain closure from the past, reading and writing is a therapeutic process. The experience raises one's self-esteem, confidence, and awareness of self.

I learned this when I created the first book in the *A Journey Of Riches* series, which is, now one of seventeen books with over 180 different co-authors from thirty-six different countries. It's not easy to write about your own personal experiences and I honor and respect every one of the authors who has collaborated in the series thus far.

For many of the authors, English is their second language, which is a significant achievement in itself. In curating this anthology of short stories, I have been touched by the amount of generosity, gratitude, and shared energy that this experience has given everyone.

The inspiration for *A Journey Of Riches, In Search of Happiness* came from my own experience of looking, seeking my own happiness and never really knowing what I was looking for exactly. Yes, I hear you say happiness comes from within, its a choice and all the other cliches. Of course, I could not have created this book without the twelve other co-authors who each said YES when I asked them to share their insights and wisdom into their journey of happiness. Just like each chapter in this book makes for inspiring reading, each story represents one chapter in the presence of each of the authors, with the chief aim of having you, the reader, living a more abundant life.

I'd like to thank all the authors for entrusting me with their unique memories, encounters, and wisdom. Thank you for sharing and opening the door to your soul so that others may learn from your experience, may the readers glean confidence from your successes and wisdom from your failures.

Thank you to my family, I know you are proud of me and how far I have come from that 10-year-old boy who was learning how to read and write at a fundamental level. Mom, Robert, Dad, Merril, my brother Adam and his daughter Krystal, my sister Hollie, her partner Brian, my nephew Charlie and my niece, Heidi. Also my grandparents Gran and Pop who are alive and well and Ma and Pa who now rest in peace. They accept me just the way I am with all my travels and adventures around the world.

Thanks to all the team at MotionMediaInternational who have done an excellent job at editing and collating this book. It has been a pleasure working with you all on this successful project, and I thank you for your patience in dealing with the various changes and adjustments along the way.

Thank you, the reader for having the courage to look at your life and how you can improve your future in a fast and rapidly changing world.

And I'd enjoy connecting with readers, as I love sharing stories. You can email me here: jrspender7@gmail.com

Thank you again to my fellow co-authors: Gabriela D Delgadillo, Peter Mcintosh, Melissa Barkell, Konstantin Doepping, Ritu Bali, Heather M. Bleakman, Sadie Konrad, Annette Forsythe, Beth Lydia RANCHEZ, Meredith Voigt Hartigan, Elizabeth Boag and Irene Cop.

I hope you have enjoyed this co-authored experience as much as I have.

With gratitude,

John Spender

"A must-read for anyone facing major changes or challenges in life right now. This book will give you the courage to move through any challenge with confidence, grace, and ease."
~ Jo-Anne Irwin - Transformational Coach & Best Selling Author.

"I'm a fan of self-help books, and I read them a lot. I love this book and the stories that are contained within them, but most of all I like the concept. I love that John Spender decided to do an anthology of stories from inspirational people. This book is the type of book where you can either choose to be inspired by ten different stories or choose a chapter that resonates with you the most.

As I read this book, it confirmed to me my life suspicion that things happen beyond our control. It can be incredibly devastating at times. It is those moments that bring us to our knees not knowing whether we can or even want to stand anymore. But, in these challenging moments, this book confirms to me that we do have one choice we can let go, make changes and embrace the new. It's the choice of how we decide to view these hardships. Our perspective determines what our life will be after these moments in our lives.

Some very heart-wrenching stories were contained in these books. Some of them I even had to ask myself, "How do you even recover from a situation like that?"

Perspective. It all boils down to how we decide to view those hard challenges that come our way. At least that is what I took away from this book.

Thank you to John and his team of authors for getting together to create this book."
~ Kit Zakimi on Amazon.

"I have enjoyed the *Journey of Riches* book series. Each person's story is written from the heart and everyone's journey different. We all have a story to tell, and John Spender does an amazing job of finding authors and combining their stories, into uplifting books."
~ Liz Misner Palmer, Foreign Service Officer.

"A timely read as I'm facing a few changes right now. I liked the various insights from the different authors. This book will inspire you to move through any challenge or change that you are experiencing."
~ David Ostrand, Business Owner.

"I've known John Spender for a while now, and I was blessed with an opportunity to be in book four in the series. I know that you will enjoy this new journey like the rest of the books in the series. The collection of stories will assist you with making changes, to deal with challenges and to see that transformation is possible for your life."
~ Charlie O'shea, Entrepreneur.

"*A Journey of Riches* series will draw you in and help you dig deep into your soul. Every author has an unbelievable life story of purpose inside of them. John Spender is dedicated to bringing peace, love, and adventure to the world of his readers! Dive into this series, and you will be transformed!!"
~ Jeana Matichak, Author of *Finding Peace*.

"Awesome! Truly inspirational! It is amazing what the human spirit can achieve and overcome! Highly recommended!!"
~ Fabrice Beliard, Australian Business Coach, and Best Selling Author.

"*A Journey of Riches* Series is a must read. It is an empowering collection of inspirational and moving stories full of courage, strength, and heart. Bringing peace and awareness to those lucky enough to read to assist and inspire them on their life journey."
~ Gemma Castiglia, Avalon Healing, Best Selling Author.

"The *A Journey of Riches* book series is an inspirational collection of books that will empower you to take on any challenge or change in life."
~ Kay Newton, Midlife Stress Buster, and Best Selling Author.

"*A Journey of Riches* book series is an inspiring collection of stories, sharing many different ideas and perspectives on how to overcome challenges, deal with change and to make empowering choices in your life. Open the book anywhere and let your mood chose where you need to read. Buy one of the books today; you'll be glad that you did! "
~ Trish Rock, Modern Day Intuitive, Bestselling Author, Speaker, Psychic & Holistic Coach.

"Transformational Change is another inspiring read in the *A Journey of Riches* book series. The authors are from all over the world, and each has a unique perspective to share, that will have you thinking differently about your current circumstances in life. An inspiring read!"
~ Alexandria Calamel, Success Coach and Best Selling Author.

"The *A Journey of Riches* books is a collection of real-life stories, which are truly inspiring and give you the confidence that no matter what you are dealing with in your life, that there is a light at the end of the tunnel, and a very bright one at that.

Totally empowering!"
~ John Abbott, Freedom Entrepreneur.

"An amazing collection of true stories from individuals who have overcome great changes and who have transformed their lives and used their experience to uplift, inspire and support others."
~ Carol Williams, Author-Speaker-Coach.

"You can empower yourself from the power within this book, that can help awaken the sleeping giant within you. John has a purpose in life to bring inspiring people together to share their wisdom, for the benefit of all who venture deep into this book Transformational Change. If you are looking for inspiration to be someone special in this book can be your guide."
~ Bill Bilwani, Renown Melbourne Restaurateur.

"In the *A Journey Of Riches* series, you will catch the impulse to step up, reconsider and settle for only the very best for yourself and those around you. Penned from the heart and with an unflinching drive to make a difference for the good of all, *A Journey Of Riches* series is a must-read."
~ Steve Coleman Author of *Decisions, Decisions! How to Make the Right One Every Time.*

"If you want to be on top of your game? *A Journey of Riches* is a must read with breakthrough insights that will help you do just that!"
~ Christopher Chen, Entrepreneur.

"In *A Journey of Riches*, you will find the insight, resources, and tools you need to transform your life. By reading the authors stories, you too can be inspired to achieve your greatest accomplishments and what is truly possible for you. Reading

this book activates your true potential for transforming, you're life way beyond what you think is possible. Read it and learn how you too can have a magical life."
~ Elaine Mc Guinness, Bestselling Author of *Unleash Your Authentic Self!*

"If you are looking for an inspiring read look no further than the *A Journey Of Riches* book series. The books are an inspiring collection of short stories, that will encourage you to embrace life even more. I highly recommend you read one of the books today!"
~ Kara Dono, Doula, Healer and Best Selling Author.

"*A Journey of Riches* series is a must-read for anyone seeking to enrich their own lives and gain wisdom through the wonderful stories of personal empowerment & triumphs over life's challenges. I've given several copies to my family, friends, and clients to inspire and support them to step into their greatness. I highly recommend that you read these books, savoring the many aha's and tools you will discover inside."
~ Michele Cempaka, Hypnotherapist, Shaman, Transformational Coach & Reiki Master.

"If you are looking for an inspirational read, look no further than the *A Journey Of Riches* book series. The books are an inspiring and educational collection of short stories from the author's soul itself, that will encourage you to embrace life even more. I've even given them to my clients too so that they are inspired by their journeys in life, wealth, health and everything else in between.

I recommend you make it a priority, to read one of the books today!"
~ Goro Gupta, Chief Education Officer, Mortgage Terminator, Property Mentor.

"The *A Journey Of Riches* book series is filled with real-life short stories of heartfelt tribulations turned into uplifting, self-transformation by the power of the human spirit to overcome adversity. The journeys captured in these books will encourage you to embrace life in a whole new way.

I highly recommend reading this inspiring anthology series."
~ Chris Drabenstott, Best Selling Author, and Editor.

"There is so much motivational power in the *A Journey of Riches* series!! Each book is a compilation of inspiring, real-life stories by several different authors, which makes the journey feel more relatable and success more attainable. If you are looking for something to move you forward, you'll find it in one (or all) of these books."
~ Cary MacArthur, Personal Empowerment Coach

"I've been fortunate to write with John Spender and now call him a friend. *A Journey of Riches* book series features real stories that have inspired me and will inspire you. John has a passion for finding amazing people from all over the world, giving the series a global perspective on relevant subject matters."
~ Mike Campbell, Fat Guy Diary, LLC

"The *A Journey of Riches* series, is the reflection of beautiful souls who have discovered the fire within. Each story takes you inside the truth of what truly matters in life. While reading these stories, my heart space expanded to understand that our most significant contribution in this lifetime is to give and receive love. May you also feel inspired as you read this book."
~ Katie Neubaum, Author of *Transformation Calling*.

"*A Journey of Riches* is an inspiring testament that love and gratitude are the secret ingredients to living a happy and fulfilling life. This series is sure to inspire and bless your life in a big way. Truly an inspirational read, written and created by real people, sharing real-life stories about the power and courage of the human spirit."
~ Jen Valadez, Emotional Intuitive, and Best Selling Author

TABLE OF CONTENTS

PREFACE

I created this book and chose this collection of authors to share their insights, into their journey of developing courage, assisting people and raising your belief that you too can tap into courage and overcome your fears.

Like all of us, each author has a unique story and insight to share with you. It just may be the case, that one or more of these authors have lived through an experience that is similar to circumstances in your life right now. Their words could be just the words you need to read to help you through your challenges and motivate you to continue on your journey. Perhaps reading about one or more of these experiences will fill in the missing piece of your puzzle, so to speak, allowing you to move forward into the next phase of your life.

Storytelling has been the way humankind has communicated ideas and learning throughout our civilization. While we have become more sophisticated with technology and living in the modern world is more convenient, there is still much discontent and dissatisfaction with one's reality. Many people have also moved away from reading books, and they are missing out on valuable information that can help them to move forward in life, with a positive outlook. I think it is essential to turn off the T.V., to slow down, and to read, reflect, and take the time to appreciate everything you have in life.

I like anthology books because they carry many different perspectives and insights on a singular topic. I find that sometimes when I'm reading a book that has just one author I gain an understanding of their viewpoint and writing style very quickly and the reading becomes predictable. With this book and all of the books in the *A Journey of Riches* book series, you have many different writing styles and viewpoints that will help shape your perspective towards your current set of circumstances.

Anthology books are also great because you can start from any chapter and gain a valuable insight or a nugget of wisdom without the feeling that you have missed something from the earlier chapters.

I love reading many different types of personal development books because learning and personal growth are vital to me. If you are not learning and growing, well, you're staying the same. Everything in the universe is growing, expanding, and changing. If we are not open to different ideas and different ways of thinking and being, then we can become close-minded.

The concept of this book series is to open you up to different ways of perceiving your reality, to give you hope, to encourage you, and to give you many avenues of thinking about the same subject. My wish for you is to feel empowered to make a decision that will best suit you in moving forward with your life. As Albert Einstein said, **"We cannot solve problems with the same level of thinking that created them."**

With Einstein's words in mind, let your mood pick a chapter in the book or read from the beginning to the end and allow yourself to be guided to find the answers you seek.

With gratitude,

John Spender

"Happiness isn't something that depends on our surroundings, it's something that we make inside ourselves."

~ Corrie Ten Boom

CHAPTER ONE

Happiness is an Inside Job

By John Spender

There I was under the bright lights in the centre of the ring with the cheers of the crowd echoing in my ears and a young lion standing in front of me trying to take my head off. This wouldn't be most people's idea of having fun, nor would you say that happiness can be found in a boxing ring. For me the opposite was true; it was the challenge of boxing and out-thinking my opponent that hooked me the most. There is a fair amount of satisfaction to be found in pursuing a goal that is bigger than ourselves. It was the year 2000 when I was recovering from the loss of my business and a severe cocaine habit that had derailed my life. I was still working for myself but doing only small residential landscaping jobs. Every afternoon I would go to the North Sydney Police Boys Club to learn the fundamentals of boxing.

At times it was grueling with all the different exercises: the heavy bag, skipping rope, speed ball, floor to ceiling ball, sit-ups, push-ups, sprints, and of course the terrifying sparring. The old school trainer was as tough as nails and looked like a character straight out of a *Rocky* movie. Well into his 50s, Tony slurred his words a little from taking too many blows to the head. He lived and breathed boxing, he was all about doing the hard yards. He had a back like a cobra, always looking ready to strike, and short back and sides crop of blackish-grey hair, sporting a nose that looked like it had been hit with a shovel (obviously from all the rounds of boxing). He was a solid man with broad, square shoulders and a thick neck. He was well-mannered, loyal to his boxing troupe, and most of all, he loved boxing. His gym was covered with memorabilia of the past greats. He was an old-school trainer and his gym had character.

"If you want to live a happy life, tie it to a goal, not to people or things."

~ Albert Einstein

My first introduction to the rough justice of Tony's ways came in my first week of training. About ten of us were touch sparring. It was my first time, I didn't really know what I was doing, although I had my fair share of fights at school, and my dad and various step-dads were also heavy-handed at times. I wasn't exactly a stranger to fighting or having to protect myself, but the sweet science of boxing was definitely different than street fighting. My limited understanding of touch sparring was that you just touched or missed your opponent. My second session was with an older guy who had been there longer than I had and was keen to exert his dominance over me. The problem was he was knee high to a grass hopper. I stand at 193 cm or 6'4" — as he rushed in with intensity, I kept catching him a little harder than a touch. Naturally, the guy took a disliking to it and complained. Tony stepped in and asked me, "You want a real spar, do you?", and before I knew what I was getting myself into, I replied "Sure!" Tony muttered, "Live by the sword, die by the sword," and he called in the most experienced boxer in the gym, an English fellow named Shane.

My first ever spar was a disaster, and under the circumstances, I should have known better. I generally go for the sink or swim approach to most things that I experience and learn in life. I felt like Neo from *The Matrix* movie when he attempts to leap across the chasm between two buildings, and, of course, he lands flat on his face. I learned that if I was going to take boxing seriously I needed more training. I also discovered the value of having a goal to strive for and pursue with a single-minded focus. The experience strengthened my resolve to have and win at least one amateur boxing match. Shane was a good-looking lad, a little shorter than myself with a shaved head and one or two basic tattoos on his arms; he looked like a no-nonsense type of guy with an air of intelligence about him. Although I never received the bloodied nose, nor did I land flat on my face, I did receive a boxing lesson from the hands of that English gent. He was incredibly fast, his ability to bridge the gap between being in and out of punching range was unbelievable. I never laid a glove on him, such was his speed and agility. The first thing to go were my legs — they had no stamina — and once they go, it's just a matter of time before you get laid out. The hard exterior of Tony cracked and he stepped in before I was seriously hurt. I did take a few blows to the head but nothing too serious. I found out later that Shane was a middle weight, and this sparring experience would be the first of many that I would have with him, that initially resulted in me being slightly concussed afterwards.

"Don't put the key to your happiness in someone else's pocket."

~ Chinmayananda Saraswati

7

Tony had a rule that was very clear. Before you had your first amateur bout you needed at least six months of experience and training under your belt. This way he could make sure that you had the necessary fitness and skills required to have a decent go of it. He didn't want to look bad either; after all, Tony's reputation was also on the line. As you can imagine, I became very fit. I naturally leaned towards healthier foods with a clear goal of staying out of trouble and more importantly, away from recreational drugs. Boxing also helped me gain some much needed confidence that had taken a blow with my failed landscaping company, having lost all the major contracts that I had worked so hard to win. I quickly rose through the ranks in the Police Boys Club to become one of the top dogs in Tony's gym which meant I had a target on my head and everyone wanted to knock it off. We started to see less and less of Shane after I gave him a bit of a touch up one evening when I caught him with a solid right hand that left him with a swollen eye that undoubtedly turned black the next day. It saddened me a little that he quit the gym; he may have received pressure from work as a result of his black eye, being an accountant for a large firm in the City Business District of North Sydney. When you have people who bring out the best of you, naturally you want to keep them around. I really wanted to improve my skills, and that English guy brought the best out of me. I was happy with the progress that I was making, the challenging part was beating up the other guys that came straight at me with aggression. This didn't bring a lot of satisfaction, especially if they were bleeding all over the place. I'm a tall, skinny guy and I don't look like a boxer at all, so when I'm sparring with a big, muscly dude, often times they don't want to look bad so they kept coming, unable to land a single blow, getting all messed up in the process.

The time had come for my first amateur boxing bout at South Sydney Junior Leagues Club. My sister was coming to watch, as well as many of my new friends that I had made at the boxing gym. I was fighting at light heavy weight, which was between 75kg-81kg, or 165-178 pounds. I didn't have to diet to make weight, I was right on the limit of 81kg. Boxing at middle weight could've been possible but Tony didn't believe in dieting or cutting weight before a bout. Being super fit it wasn't uncommon to have a cold, as one's immune system can be weakened by the strenuous training routines, and I had a slight bug on fight night. Still brimming with confidence, mostly because I had excellent strength, my skill level had improved dramatically from my conditioning. I had a strong left jab and a powerful straight right. The last six months had been just what I needed to gain order and structure in my life, not to mention the discipline to show up week after week to the often punishing sessions. No matter what happened in my ensuing bout, I could be proud of myself for turning my life around. Through dedicating a lot of time and hard work to my goal, training six days a week, I felt quite confident. An hour or so before the fight, Tony received intel that although it was technically my opponent's first official amateur bout with the Australian Amateur Boxing Association, he was in fact the light heavy weight Australian Navy champion. It wasn't the best news to come moments before my first fight, but I was still confident of winning. I had sparred many amateurs that were experienced and had held my own against them.

"A deep sense of happiness can come from pursuing a vision bigger than ourselves."

~ Anonymous

There I was in the centre of the ring under the bright lights with the cheers of the crowd echoing in my ears, and above all, I could hear my good friend Jake screaming at the top of his lungs, "Go Spender, you've got this!" As soon as the bell rang, we both immediately attacked with straight left jabs; his landed on my right glove so hard that I hit myself in the face. We were wearing 10oz gloves compared to the 16oz gloves we wore in training — if you weren't careful, you could easily get knocked out. The young lion was compact with well-defined muscles, evident through his blue singlet; he had a resolve of steel and he had come to win. He was trying to double jab his way into contact range, but lucky for me, I have long arms — 195cm from finger tip to finger tip — and with a piston-like jab, it was hard for my shorter opponent to get into my guard without getting caught once or twice. Tony's strategy was simple attack with my jab, defend with my right, and if an opening appeared, drive home the right hand. If you managed to get inside my jab, I would throw a right upper cut followed by a left hook. The latter was a new combination that I had only been practicing for a couple of weeks, so I wasn't as confident with this combination. The first round was close; it wasn't until the second round that I caught the Navy champ with a well-timed double left right combination that left him hanging on the ropes. I lacked the killer instinct to finish him off, and when I watched the replay, I saw that after I had hurt him, I began unconsciously looping my right hand punches, reducing their impact. At the core of my being, I was soft, sensitive, and I didn't want to hurt anyone. The Navy champ, on the other hand, came back strong in the last round and wanted to win at any cost. He threw everything but the kitchen sink at me as I danced around the ring. The last round was close and he started slipping my jabs and banging me with his left hook. I was side-stepping his ferocious attacks forward. My opponent's intensity was so great that after one charge forward as he bobbed and weaved throwing punches, I swiveled out of the way and he went flying through the ropes, almost landing on the judges table.

Only two weeks earlier, Tony had taken the other boxers and me through a goal-setting exercise to set goals for what we would like to achieve as boxers. For me, boxing was a tool to help with my emotional state. Having one bout seemed like a good goal to have, but I was afraid to tell Tony, as he often told me I could be state champion in a year or two. Not wanting to disappoint him, I wrote down that I would like to be state champion as a goal. In truth, that was his goal, not mine, and after the fight, I knew for sure that I didn't want to box anymore. Who wants to get punched in the face anyway?

What I learned in a nutshell:

1.) I learned that you can't expect to be happy if you're making decisions to please other people. Most definitely, no lasting, fulfilling happiness will be birthed by setting goals because you believe it'll make someone else happy.

2.) If you set a goal for yourself, you best set another one after you achieve it to avoid any empty feelings. It really does help to have a goal to look forward to in life.

3.) Winning isn't everything and goals become more meaningful when they are attached to a strong sense of purpose — something greater than yourself.

"Those that mind, don't matter and those that matter don't mind."

~ Dr. Seuss

After three two-minute rounds, the announcer had the judges' scores. I looked over to my challenger, his face was a bloody mess; it didn't feel good at all. His right eye was swollen, bruised and was almost closed, he had a cut lip, and he had red marks all over his face. When the announcer said "And the winner by the narrowest of margins..." I instantly thought 'Oh no, the judges have rewarded his aggressive never say die effort.' The announcer continued, "And the winner from the red corner, John Spender!" I had won the fight, but surprisingly, I felt empty inside. The fulfillment and happiness that I had experienced came from the pursuit of my goal, not the achievement of it.

I decided to replace boxing with tropical fish. I won $700 on the poker machines in my local pub after watching a Ruby League match where my team, the West Tigers, had just won. I played the pokies once in a blue moon — something drew me to them as I went to leave, maybe because I was feeling good after the Tigers won. Anyway, I put $20 in a dollar machine and hit the jackpot. The next day I bought a top quality aquarium. I used to breed tropical fish when I was a youngster and this experience helped me transition away from boxing, giving me something to do after work. I enjoy sitting and watching the fish swim in the tank and observing the various personalities from species to species. I still did a boxercise class run by a different trainer. There was no sparring involved and the sessions were focused on boxing skill and fitness which was fun. Tony took my quitting as rejection; he was visibly disappointed and wanted nothing to do with me, but that's ok… sometimes you have to risk disappointing another so you can do what is right for you, ultimately putting your own happiness first.

What is Your Definition of Happiness?

No doubt, happiness means different things depending on the beliefs of the individual. One of the best definitions I have found is by Tony Hsieh, the CEO of Zappos, a successful online shoe and clothing company. Well-known for building an incredible team culture and exceptional customer service, he shares his entrepreneurial journey as CEO in his book *Delivering Happiness: A Path to Profits, Passion and Purpose*. His take on happiness has stuck with me ever since I read the book. Hsieh breaks happiness down into three forms, the first being the happiness that comes from instant gratification. You can buy a new car or go out to your favourite restaurant, but the experience has no real meaning and is short lived. The second form of happiness is around the pursuit and achievement of goals. This form of happiness lasts for a little longer than the first. Finally, the third form of happiness is in creating a vision bigger than yourself that makes a difference beyond your own immediate gain.

"Life is not something that has meaning - it's something that we give meaning to. You don't end up with a meaningful life, you create it."

~ Unknown

Hsieh's definition has helped me prioritise my activities, and is part of the reason that all the royalties from the *A Journey Of Riches* books are donated to charity. We have been supporting the Bali Street Kids Project for two years now, and I'm filled with a deeper sense of purpose when I put these books together, knowing that the authors and I are collectively making a difference to the orphans of Bali. They are clothed, fed, educated, and have a roof over their heads. The books are a well of happiness that keep on giving. The *A Journey of Riches* project is a win-win-win: for the authors who go through the therapeutic process of sharing from a place of vulnerability, for the reader who gets to read positive, inspiring stories, and of course, for the children.

My definition of happiness may be completely different from yours, but when you find what has deep meaning for you and fulfill that meaning, you live with purpose and increase your ability to have longer-lasting happiness. Above all else, it's important to do what brings you joy inside, not what your parents or peers think is best for you. In all likelihood, this may mean doing the the thing that people will call you crazy for pursuing; but if you don't put your happiness first, then how can you be truly happy?

George Lucas, the creator and director of the box office phenomenon *Star Wars,* has an interesting take on happiness. He believes there are two forms of happiness: pleasure and joy. He gave a speech about his life and the journey of becoming a successful film-maker. He shared the pitfall that he side-stepped by rejecting his father's recommendation of working full-time selling office furniture for the family business. Lucas knew he would hate that, and his father was naturally disappointed. After he shared his journey to success, Lucas went on to explain that pleasure is represented by the money, fancy cars, and big house. Not only is the feeling of happiness short-lived, to gain that same feeling of happiness, you will need to buy bigger and better things to sustain it. The appetite for this form of happiness is never-ending. The best form of happiness is joy, which isn't as strong of a feeling as pleasure but it's easier to achieve and can be found in the simplest of things. Choose joy over pleasure is the advice from George Lucas. I have to agree that joy, although at times subtle, is the well of spring water that never runs dry. Pursue joy and happiness is sure to follow.

Travel for me has been a great source of happiness. I love the excitement of visiting a new place, the process of adapting to new surroundings, the different types of foods, and of course, all the cultural nuances. My interest is spiked when I see another's travel photos. I also like to read travel adventure books. One of the books I'm reading at the moment is *Africa Solo* by Mark Beaumont, about his pursuit of the world record as the fastest person to ride unassisted from Cairo to Cape Town. The book has peaks, valleys, and triumphs, and tells of how Mark finds appreciation in the smallest of things. I've only started reading it and it's fascinating how cruising down the highway in Egypt with a tail wind propelling him forward could produce feelings of satisfaction.

"Gross national happiness is more important than gross national product."

~Jigme Singye Wangchuck

A close friend is currently traveling through Bhutan visiting monasteries, hiking up mountains, and soaking in hot baths after a long day of hiking. I thought of how I would like to visit Bhutan and experience the culture, the incredible monasteries perched on the side of cliff faces, and a strong, religious backbone of Buddhism. Bhutan is also famous for creating 'gross national happiness' where they measure the happiness of the people. The idea came from former King,

Jigme Singye Wangchuck. Upon seeing how other countries
are run around the central theme of economic growth, he
dreamed of a different model for his people. His challenge
became how to balance economic abundance and happiness.
The King based his decisions on one question: will this bring
happiness to the people? In 2006, the King resigned and
made his son King at the ripe old age of 16. The vision was
to hand the power back to the people, and the country had
its first democratic election in 2008. The new government
used questionnaires and polls to assess the happiness of its
people. What they found was that if the people had shared
interests with others, such as hobbies, participating in
cultural activities, preserving customs and cultural heritage,
they felt like they belonged to a meaningful community and
were happy. In addition, having clear values and a definite
sense of identity while belonging to a community were key
factors contributing to a person's level of happiness. The UN
conducts a study every year with the intent of ascertaining
which countries are the happiest. They gather data relating
to GDP, level of corruption, social services, healthy life
expectancy, freedom to make life choices, and generosity.
Surprisingly, their research has established Finland as the
happiest country in the world. The Finns scored well on all
factors and especially high on generosity, which goes to show
that helping others really does make you feel better. The
study showed that almost half of Finns consistently donate to
charity and one-third said they regularly volunteer their time
to various charities.

It's worth noting that Finland doesn't have the highest GDP,
and according to research by Forbes Magazine, Finland is the
13th best country for doing business. The country is known
for its strong social services, freedom of choice, and positive

work-life balance. Finland is an example that you don't have to be the richest country in the world to be the happiest.

"We make a living by what we get, but we make a life by what we give."

~ Winston Churchill

Recently on my travels to Kuala Lumpur, I was speaking to my friend Darren Weiler about creating the idea for this book, and he said he had read an interesting article about the five biggest regrets of the dying. Darren made a good point that what we don't do says a lot about our state of happiness. After doing a bit of research, I found an interesting article in *The Guardian* about the book *The Top Five Regrets of the Dying* written by an ex-nurse, Bronnie Ware, who worked in palliative care for several years. Ware spent the last months with dying patients and recorded their moments of clarity and what they would do differently. Following are the top five regrets of the dying, according to Bronnie's observations:

1. I wish I'd had the courage to live a life true to myself, not the life others expected of me.

This was the typical regret from people who discovered that they were going to die without playing their music. It was easy to see that they had lived someone else's dream and not their own. In many cases, it's the people closest to us who apply the most pressure to fulfill the life that *they* feel is best for us. Just like my boxing trainer who was disappointed that I didn't follow *his* version of my best life. You have to stand up for your own happiness and set clear boundaries, otherwise your life may end up being a lie. I've lost count how many times I've had to disappoint my parents so I can stay true to myself, and now they accept me just the way I am. That wasn't always easy. Standing up for your dreams (and ultimately your happiness) takes courage.

2. I wish I hadn't worked so hard.

Ware was quoted in the *Guardian* as saying that every male patient she spoke with regretted working too hard. I'm not sure if this is one of my dad's regrets, but he wasn't there to watch us grow up and he certainly wasn't there for my mom when she needed him most. All too often we get caught on the hamster wheel of work, only to eek out a barley modest life with too many Monday blues, hump days, and thank God it's Fridays. In many cases, people live far beyond their means, buying things they don't really need. The answer may well be in simplifying your life and turning your passion into your career. People will rarely, if ever regret not working hard enough.

3. I wish I'd have had the courage to express my feelings.

Not expressing how you really feel breeds resentment and disease. Most people don't like conflict and won't express how they truly feel just to keep the peace. As a whole, we play it safe rather than risk being vulnerable, and bottling up emotions is definitely most common with the older generation. I believe today's generation is much more expressive with their feelings. When we express what's important, we are more readily able to live up to our highest potential.

4. I wish I had stayed in touch with my friends.

Even with social media there is a major disconnect between people today, which is strange, as it's never been easier to keep in touch with friends. You may think that the millennial generation won't have this regret when they're on their death beds with all the social interactions online. You may be right, but the regret might sound more like "I wish I would have caught up with my friends through more face-to-face interactions rather than through social media and text messaging." What we give our time to is a clear indication of what we value. Even as busy as I am, I make it a point to have two or three in-person friend catch ups every week.

5. I wish that I had let myself be happier.

Many people don't realise that happiness is in fact a choice. It's quite astounding how many people believe that happiness is found outside of themselves. Seeking happiness from outside forces produces the kind of happiness that just doesn't last and can result in addictive behaviours. As we grow older, there is a tendency to forget how to laugh and have fun, just for the sake it. Laughter is the best medicine and most of us can increase the daily dose.

"Happiness is not something that you postpone for the future; it is something you design for the present"

~ Jim Rohn

As Jim Rohn said, you are responsible for the level of happiness that you are experiencing in your life. You can experience happiness through spontaneous action, getting involved in hobbies, chatting with good friends, pursuing a goal or vision, meditating and connecting with yourself, and countless other ways. Our brains are designed to keep us alive, not to bring happiness; that's your job. At the end of the day, happiness is a choice. I knew boxing was no longer going to bring me happiness. A decision needed to be made or my well being and metal state over the long term would decline and my soul would surely die a slow death. Lasting happiness can rarely be reached by putting other peoples needs before your own. When you protect your happiness, it will always be with you. You'll no longer need to chase happiness, it will follow you wherever you go.

"Everyone wants happiness, no one wants pain, but you can't have a rainbow without a little rain."

~ Unknown

CHAPTER TWO

A JOURNEY TO HAPPINESS OUT OF THE DARKNESS AND INTO THE LIGHT

By Gabriela Delgadillo

Mexico City: The Breakdown

I boarded Delta flight 945 destined for Mexico City. I looked out the aircraft window and saw the unbelievably expansive, all-embracing city I knew so well. I began to feel a slight uneasiness but at the same time, an incredible feeling of exhilaration. I could catch a glimpse of the Popocatepetl's smoking cone, the floating gardens of Xochimilco, the bustle of the city dwellers living life. Rich memories welled up in me of floating across the waters in a gondola, mariachi music in the air, the smell of jasmine in bloom. I saw through the veil of murkiness and polluted fog, excited to be returning to the magic of the city — the ancient city of the Aztecs, Tenochtitlan.

I moved there temporarily to help open up the Latin market for a multi-billion-dollar international company. I rented a four-bedroom penthouse in downtown Mexico City in the posh neighborhood of Reforma. The view from my bedroom window faced the golden image of the famous Angel of

Independence. I had a chauffeur that was at my beck and call, a housekeeper, and a naturopathic doctor that made house calls when the need arose. I had a massage therapist that came twice a week and a spiritual Shaman who was my trusted advisor. I was living a life that most people only dream about. I traveled all over the world both for business and pleasure. But there was one thing missing. I was not happy. I was self-absorbed.

I had worked myself into a mania while living in Mexico City. I couldn't sleep, I was getting anxiety attacks because I was doing too much. I was going too fast and my life started to unravel in a downward spiral of events, eventually pushing me over the edge. My ex-husband of 25 years ran off with my brother's wife, my daughter narrowly survived a heroin overdose, the company I was consulting for went bankrupt, and my significant other went into rehab. My mind just couldn't handle the stress. I had a nervous breakdown. I now call it my break-through! This was a critical component in my journey into discovering my true, authentic self and my real purpose in life.

I passed out on the sidewalk in front of my penthouse building where my boyfriend Francisco found me. He called an ambulance that took me to the hospital. When I got there, I was disoriented and confused. Before this, I had gone to see a psychiatrist because I was starting to experience depression from the stress that was piling up on me. He put me on an antidepressant that possibly caused a manic episode. In other words, it got me out of the depression but caused the mania.

I was taken to an elite behavioral health hospital in Mexico City, The Hospital Español. I was immediately given antipsychotic medications, as they assumed that I had a manic episode and needed to bring me down. The cocktail that I was administered sent me on a frightening hallucination trip. I was terrified — the delusions and paranoia were so real to me. My mother was notified, and she immediately flew to Mexico to be by my side. Together with Francisco, they were my advocates and worked with the doctors to stabilize me enough to get back to my permanent home in Phoenix, AZ. To travel in my unstable and heavily-medicated state, I was placed on a stretcher and it was required that I be accompanied by a medical doctor who never left my side and regularly administered medication. That flight alone depleted my already dwindling resources by $15,000. When I arrived in Phoenix, an ambulance was there at the airport waiting to take me to Banner Health Behavioral Hospital.

Despite all the precautions, I was still in a crisis state when I arrived. My blood pressure was out of control and I was shaking uncontrollably from side effects of the medications. My speech was slurred, and I was unable to let anyone know how terrified and lost I felt. I tried to communicate by touching my thumb and my index finger together, thinking they could understand, but it was just in my imagination. Francisco worked with the doctors to get me stabilized. He insisted they administer something to bring my blood pressure down and a muscle relaxant so I would stop shaking. A few hours later I felt some peace.

After about two weeks at Banner, one of the medications I was taking caused aggressive behavior. I threatened and bullied the staff and my peers. Eventually, this led to my reassignment to the UPC (Urgent Psychiatric Crisis Response Center). Drugged and delusional, I was forced into a police cruiser attended by a Police K9 trained to bite.

Dancing in The Dark

I don't belong here! Please take me home! I am not a homeless person!," I raved. "I haven't done anything wrong," I shouted, as my eyes filled with tears and two policemen escorted me into what appeared to be a hell hole psychiatric jail. I screamed and raged, causing a few people to glance at me with the look of detachment, likely thinking 'Just another psych patient gone wild.' At that moment, I became unhinged. I was intensely confused and disconcerted. I looked around at the nauseating, stench-filled, open hall filled with very strange people. I felt utterly visible and exposed to everyone. There were no private rooms, no curtains, nowhere to hide. Some people were wearing hospital gowns which exposed their most intimate parts. This was a scary and repugnant place. I felt that my life had become a broken-winged bird, unable to fly. Why was I here? I became increasingly anxious and agitated when no one would respond to my queries. Everyone just gawked at me with their bewildered faces. Some were delirious, others were ranting, and others were just trying to sleep. I thought, 'I am in jail! But what did I do? What crime did I commit?' I would never have dreamt in a million years that I could experience something like this. After all, I had been a highly-functioning, intelligent, talented, and rich woman. This sort of thing doesn't happen to people like me. Well, it does, and it did.

Yes, I have tasted the bitter and the sweet in life. I have had great success in many areas of my life but, clearly, I have also had my share of failures and despair. The waves of adversity came crashing at my door with fierceness, but deep within all of us lies a foundation which remains as firm as a rock amidst the storm. In despair, it's hard to understand how you can possibly get to the other side of the trials that befall you. There is always a way; I can attest to that. We can overcome adversity and achieve happiness. Finding the right support through family, friends, and significant others was crucial on my journey. I'm grateful to my blessed mother who was by my side every step of the way, and thankful for her undying sacrifice during my crisis. I'm also thankful for my significant other, Francisco, for not losing hope that I would come back from the abyss.

I have learned that the universal Principle of Rhythm encompasses the truth that there is always action and reaction along the same axis of polarity. A pendulum swings from side to side, the tides of the seas ebb and flow. The sun comes out and then the moon, the seasons change. Our lives will never be stagnant, we will always be in motion. Tragedy is no respecter of persons. We have two choices: we can reach for light or die. As for me, I choose to reach for light and be happy.

Early life

When I was a child in Mexico, I dreamt of being a Flamenco dancer. I dreamt of playing the guitar, being an artist, and entertaining in front of thousands of people on a huge stage. I possessed all those qualities that make children so magical. I saw the beauty, the wonder, and miracles that were around me. I was curious, faithful, and trusting. I didn't know what 'duende' was at the time, but now I know I owned it even then. Duende means goblin or fairy, but to the flamenco artist it signifies the inner force that fuels an inspired performance. As an observer, it's not something you can see, it's that mysterious thing that makes a song or a dance something special, something amazing — a spontaneous expression of the moment's emotions.

> "Know you what it is to be a child? It is to
> believe in love, to believe in loveliness, to
> believe in belief; it is to be so little that the
> elves can reach to whisper in your ear, it is to
> turn pumpkins into coaches, and mice into
> horses, lowness into loftiness, and nothing
> into everything, for each child has its fairy
> godmother in its soul. It is to live in a nutshell
> and to count yourself the king of infinite space. It
> is to see the world in a grain of sand and Heaven
> in a wildflower. Holding infinity in the palm of
> your hand and eternity in an hour."
>
> ~ Francis Thompson

At a very tender age, I was taught by my father Rene, a true Renaissance man, that I was magical and was an alchemist who could turn lead into gold. I believed in his creative expectancy of me and spent most of my life trying to live up to his expectation. Those expectations were a double-edged sword that would take time, experience, and wisdom to balance. My father instilled in me the belief that I was capable of everything I set my mind to. Now I had to decide, through all my trials and errors, what was essential and deserving of my incredible energies. With the foundation of belief in myself and the exuberance and inexperience of youth, I became an overachiever. I accomplished many of the things I dreamt I wanted to do and then some. I came to the US when I was nine years old. I was wise beyond my years, skipped grades, and excelled in school. Graduating from high school at 15 with a full academic scholarship to college, I went on to get my education, marry well, have five beautiful children, and excel in business and as an international motivational speaker.

Success

People said she was happy, beautiful, successful, and rich. They watched as she filmed a talk show viewed by over 10 million people in 17 countries in Latin America. They followed her over the months as she trained executives, worked with housewives, and counseled CEOs. They heard her bring the house down with tears and laughter as she spoke to thousands who showed their appreciation and respect with endless applause and rising to their feet in a standing ovation. She seemed incredibly happy. How was it that this 34-year-old woman had accomplished so much in such a short period of time? That woman was me; yet somehow, I was still restless and unsatisfied. What was missing? I hadn't found myself. I had devoted myself to my husband, my children, and the acquisition of material gain.

The year was 2001. My father had just passed away. Papa never made it to Spain, the land of his ancestors, so I decided to go there in his honor. It was in Spain where I would learn to feel alive again. I was 43 years old, and that journey was the one that would change my life forever.

Rudyard Kipling wrote:

> **"People say that what we're all seeking is the meaning of life...I think that what we're really seeking is the experience of being alive."**

Spain

Land of magic and enchantment. Land of human rhythm. Land of gypsies, Flamenco, and the bullfight. Land of my ancestors.

In Spain, the light is different — hotter. The music stirs the blood. It is a land of touch and taste where the essence of everything seems at its most intense. The air is filled with the aromas of olives, jasmine, fish frying in oil, tomatoes, bitter orange, and lemon groves…the magic of dancing horses. Senses become heightened. It is a country filled with passion that understands sensuality and "duende.»

In this mythical, timeless place, I began to feel within me the renewal of the passion for life. I discovered a great desire to pursue the authentic life path which was my destiny, to gain emotional freedom and find peace, harmony, and joy, and the confidence that I had lost somewhere along the way. I began to explore my inner self and discovered the source of my restlessness. I smelled the jasmine, rode a white stallion through the countryside, and saw the sunsets in April. I thought of my father. 'You were the one who taught me that everything was possible. Thank you, Papa.'

Reach For Light or Die

I returned from Spain with a deeper understanding of myself. My life had to change to reflect that inner knowledge. My marriage could not weather the storm of my transformation into a woman who knew what she wanted for herself, perhaps for the first time since childhood. Have you ever dreamt of stepping on the sandy beaches on the other side of the world? Visiting Rome or walking down the narrow streets of Italy and Spain? As a young woman, I dreamt about it all the time. For as long as I could remember, I wanted to see the world. My outward journey finally reflected my inner travels. I spent time on the beaches of the world, saw the beautiful change of fall colors in Vermont while taking an art class from world-renowned Renaissance master artist Frank Covino. I worked under his tutelage for over a decade in the classical style of the masters with verdacio underpainting techniques and oil glazes. He told me I needed to master the classics until I earned the right to create my own style. Once I reached that milestone, I felt the deep need to create my own style, so I began to explore other mediums such as acrylics, photography, graphic and digital art. Through this process of growth and experimentation, I created a foundation that would eventually become my own mixed media technique.

I traveled the Florida Keys and visited Ernest Hemingway's home. I was enthralled and consumed by the great works of Michelangelo and Leonardo Da Vinci, visiting the great museums of Rome. I lived in a country club estate in Florida and had the blessing of taking a year sabbatical to live on the beaches of St. Augustine, the oldest City in America, in a beautiful beach house with an ocean view. All these adventures and too many others to list nourished my burgeoning artist's soul. Still running, still acquiring, still working very hard, but also loving the beauty of the world and experiencing real freedom and exploration of the soul.

In the whirlwind of travel, exploration, work, and life, I continued to strive toward many goals. Then my world seemed to implode as I was rocked with the events that shook me to my core and landed me raving in a psychiatric hospital in Phoenix, where we began this story together. My family and friends were able to secure a move from the UPC facility to a one where I could stabilize and recover. This new care center had rehabilitation classes, and I was expected to attend. All I wanted to do was sleep, as I was still doped up on prescribed drugs. In one class we were asked to make a drawing of what we were feeling at the moment. I drew a sunflower reaching over a brick wall with the sun shining that read, "Reach for light or die."

In the midst of madness, my spirit's strength and true essence showed through. I went to the nurse's station and asked if I could teach a class on vision boarding and goal setting. The nurse looked at me strangely and said, "Let me see what I can do to set it up." I called my mother and my sisters and asked if they would bring the materials. Magazines, scissors, poster paper, and glue. The day of the class arrived and I had 14 participants, all of whom suffered from some type of mental illness. I began by telling them an inspiring story about achievement. I assured them they could still dream and turn their dreams into reality. Then I explained that a vision board is something that will help you set your intentions to the Universe about what you want to accomplish. My mother and my sisters sat in awe with tears in their eyes as they witnessed me doing what I loved. Even in my psychotic state, I was able to tap into the sleeping giant inside of me that knew how to ignite a fire in others. Looking around the room, I saw a glimmer of hope in the smiles on the faces of these patients. I had everyone excited, working diligently on their vision boards. The seed of what would become my mission statement carried me through the dark hours: "I am committed to the pursuit of knowledge and to the development of my talents to help myself and others reach our full human potential in mind, body, and spirit."

New Beginnings

I woke up one day and decided to take my power back. I declared, "Enough!" The withdrawal from the antipsychotic drugs was an arduous journey that took almost a year of my life. The nights were long and scary; the nightmares didn't stop. The desperate need for air caused me great anxiety, my lungs seemed to scream for it in desperation. I was scared to fall asleep because I thought I would stop breathing and die. The pain in my head and neck were debilitating. I prayed, I meditated, I sang. I didn't want to give up on thinking there was a God somewhere that could hear my plea. I lulled myself to sleep with a song every night. Then one day my prayer was answered. The pain and anguish of it all just vanished! I felt peace for the first time in a very long time. My creative spirit was awakened and I could actually pick up a paintbrush again. I began to work fast and furious like a maniac. I started reading again. Even though I had always been an avid reader, during this crisis, I read very little because I was not able to concentrate. I began the road to recovery by delving into my art once again.

I began attending art classes and art therapy at Art Awakenings, a behavioral health art school. Ashamed, I didn't want anyone to know I was visiting, but it gave me a chance to come back to myself, to my greatness. At first, it took me a very long time to finish a painting and it didn't look very impressive. With the help of Tiffany, my art therapist, I was able to regain my confidence. I grew courageous and began to experiment with new forms of creating. I played with terracotta clay and discovered I had a natural ability to create beautiful and unique jewelry that everyone wanted. Art Awakenings began to show my work and I started to get exposure. One children's behavioral health center bought 12 of my paintings. My work took on a different meaning and style. The light came back and the colors were bright and the content deep and meaningful. I had awakened. I was once again able to tap into my creative spirit and touch the lives of many.

Later, I started volunteering at Art Awakenings and as a health and wellness coach for people with mental disabilities. I especially enjoyed working with the elderly who suffered from dementia and Alzheimer's; I could relate all too well to being lost in your own mind. One of my clients, Lorraine, was going through withdrawals from antipsychotic medications and she was shaking, crawling in her own skin, and in severe pain. She prayed that God would take her, a familiar prayer I knew well. 'I know your pain,' I thought, as I stroked her soft white hair with tears streaming down my cheeks. I said silently, "I understand — I have been where you are and I know the pain will end. I cannot take it away from you, but I can be here to give you comfort and understanding." A burden of pain is easier to bear with a kindred spirit by your side. My compassion increased, and my capacity to love unconditionally expanded beyond limits. I regained my mental health through my service to others. My creative spirit walked with me, step by step, upon my true path to happiness. As I began to see transformation take place in the lives of the clients I worked with, a real sense of purpose and joy began to well up inside me. I painted over 1000 works of art in ten years. Tapping into my passion for art transformed my life and healed me. Through art, I discovered my true, authentic journey. Along with other alternative healing modalities, I began to use art as therapy to stimulate healing to those suffering from mental illness.

"As we lose ourselves in the service of others, we discover our own lives and our own happiness."

~ Dieter F. Uchtdorf

I began to go even deeper into my art, which became more colorful, greater depth, spiritual, and had more meaning. I started to share my art on social media and in over 60 worldwide online galleries. I received rave reviews from international critics. I read emails and messages from people all over the world expressing how my art was changing their lives and reaching them deeply. I began to win international art contests. The critics were saying that I was one of the up and coming artists to watch. I was so profoundly moved because I realized how far I had come from the days when I was at Art Awakenings and struggled to begin with a brush in my hand. I was creating art that truly inspires.

The Game of Enlightenment

In the Spring of 2018, I had a dream to create a game with my art. I played a game as a child called "Loteria." It's a game similar to bingo that is played with images instead of numbers. I came up with the idea of creating a deck of cards and game board with my art and inspirational messages on the reverse side that is based on values and virtues. I added a multi-sensory component to the game that gave it depth and inspired transformation in the participants.

The Game of Enlightenment is the sum of my life's journey to this point. Combining the experiences I have had, the wisdom I have gained, the adversity I have overcome, this has led me to true happiness. The game is a stimulating collection of alternative learning in the area of Arts and Humanities, Metaphysical Studies, Universal Law, New Thought, and New Age Studies and Science. The Game of Enlightenment incorporates and integrates the dynamics of mindfulness, health and wellness, personal and interpersonal growth, love and kindness, gratitude, as well as strength-based and non-judgmental approaches of radical acceptance. The Game of Enlightenment is growing to benefit individuals in every aspect of their lives, including spiritual, psychological, and biophysical quality of life, as well as on micro and macro levels related to our connectedness with our world and the Universe. The game of enlightenment is a path to bringing care to a more significant number of people than the one-on-one of caregiving.

Through art and service, I checked back into life and gained a whole new perspective. I reduced the complexity of my life by eliminating the needless wants. I realized, as Socrates said, "The secret of happiness, you see, is not found in seeking more, but in developing the capacity to enjoy less." Gone are the Mercedes, Rolexes, and penthouse. I now enjoy the incredible beauty and simplicity of a one-bedroom cottage on a beautiful two-acre orange grove. Sometimes I have my two-year-old granddaughter as a visitor. Tucking her into bed at night, I hold her tiny hand in mine. With a soft, dry paintbrush in my other hand, I paint her hair and her face, very softly, singing her a lullaby. These simple joys are happiness for me. Touching those tiny hands, touching old wrinkled hands in caregiving, that is my happiness, my service. The gifts of the spirit have allowed me to give to others.

When you have a near death experience, everything seems to change in your life. I now realize that if I had not had that nervous breakdown, I would never have had my spiritual break-through! And I found my journey to happiness. I would not be doing what I am doing right now. Everything has arrived in perfect timing and has been Divinely inspired. I know that the Universe and God are orchestrating every detail of my life, and I've been put on the planet to serve humanity. Everything is falling into place in Divine order. My purpose and the path to my happiness are to make a difference in people's lives. Sometimes we have to hit rock bottom and be humbled to realize that there is more to life than ourselves, our possessions, and our EGOs. I now live by the adage that the things we do for ourselves die with us, and the things we do for others carry on throughout eternity.

She Came Back To Life
by Sarah L. Harvey

So she could love those tough times, she could love herself at the bottom of it all — but this did not magically make those times pretty. It did not tie them up with a pretty, pink satin bow or make the pain okay.

Nothing will really make that okay—and yet, healing is still possible. That's the gift of it all.

So in those cool, jagged underground tunnels and spaces, she cried, she learned, she healed.

She fought for her life.

She fought for her voice.

For her spirit to rise up and blossom into the fiery breathlessness of spring.

She fought so hard for so long.

And one day, she realized she did not have to fight anymore.

She knew she could summon that blazing intensity whenever she needed it, sure—but she no longer needed to fight like hell to make it through the day.

Up, up, up

She came

Out of the ground.

"I love you," she said

To that stunning, first breath of fresh air

To that patch of golden sunlight on the just-sprouting blades of lime-green grass

To the way life can look so different after the ache...

"If you want happiness for an hour - take a nap.

If you want happiness for a day - go fishing.

If you want happiness for a month - get married.

If you want happiness for a year - inherit a fortune.

If you want happiness for a lifetime - help someone else."

~ Chinese proverb

CHAPTER THREE

Our Journey to the Pyramids

By Peter Mcintosh

It all happened one Nyepi Day[1] on the Island of the Gods, Bali, six years ago.

Bali is a tranquil island blessed with a unique culture that combines both Hindu and Buddhist ceremonies, which culminate in Nyepi Day, or Silent Day. This wondrous day is celebrated every year at the beginning of March. For those of you who have only ever experienced the hustle and bustle of Bali, you would be surprised to land here on the one day of the year where everything literally comes to a complete stop. On the eve of Nyepi Day, grotesque, larger-than-life man-made characters are paraded through the streets of towns and villages, all designed to scare away the Evil Spirits. Then, from 2am, everything is shut down, including the internet and the airport. Nobody is allowed out of their homes, compounds, hotels or wherever they are staying. The streets are deserted. There are none of the normal sounds of vehicles, commerce or industry. It is the ultimate lazy quiet day!

---

1 Nyepi is a Balinese "Day of Silence" that is commemorated every Isakawarsa (Saka new year) according to the Balinese calendar

Evil spirits are lost and confused and cannot find their way home, according to the theory behind Nyepi Day, thus people stay off the streets, even televisions and lights are switched off. Everyone loves this day of serenity. Wouldn't it be so wonderful if the whole world followed suit? It's almost impossible to imagine the incredible positive flow-on effects this could have globally!

On that beautiful quiet Nyepi morning I was sitting on a small wall gazing out over the surreal setting of the Ayung River. Mist lay in the valley and swirled around the undergrowth; the brilliant blue Javanese Kingfishers swooped and dived between the majestic trees. In the background were only nature's sounds and the gentle rustling of the overhead branches of the Suara trees.

I closed my eyes and leaned back against the upright wall, I let my legs dangle over the edge far above the jungle, I placed my thumb and forefingers together and, resting on my thighs, I started my morning meditation.

Going into a meditative state was still fairly new to me. Back in 2005, my beautiful wife Lynn and I were introduced to the joy of starting a spiritual journey, as opposed to the journey of corporate and business pursuits that we had engaged in for many years of our lives. It was a gentle change at first, but one that had a profound effect on us both. In my case, it commenced when I was invited to lie down in a tipi-type building in which I heard and felt a very large symphonic gong playing.

This experience was so very different from anything else I had ever felt in my life that I was deeply affected. There was an unfamiliar stirring within me. I later came to realise that I had experienced 'Sound Healing' and it was quite amazing!

The next decade passed with us both quickly letting go of what had been so important in the past, particularly the amassing of material possessions, the corporate lifestyle and some of our supposed friendships. Soon gone were the days of pre-judging people, ego, heavy mortgages and endeavouring to demonstrate our wealth to the world. These trappings of success were replaced with a calmer and accepting attitude towards life and an awareness that other influences were guiding us constantly.

Fast forward to 2013 and I was focused on my breathing and doing my best to block out all other thoughts that seemed to be trying to interrupt this special time of relaxation. Soon I became aware of an image before me, I resisted opening my eyes and tried to discern what I was seeing. It was in fact two objects that looked like triangles joined together. As it morphed into a more identifiable picture I realised I was seeing two pyramids much like those one would expect to see on the Giza Plain of Cairo.

Suddenly I felt the hairs on my arms rise, goose bumps broke out and I perceived a very strong message – *"Peter, you are to build two pyramids here in Ubud that will be used for Sound Healing."*

Wow. I began to think that this time the Spirit had dropped in on the wrong guy! Again the images appeared, now I was looking down on the pyramids, once again another message came to me, *"No Peter this is your journey, your retirement is over"*!

I was in awe as the images slowly faded. As I opened my eyes, I looked to see if the sun was shining through the branches, creating a light image on my eyelids. That could have created an apparition of a Pyramid! But no, I was totally in the open, there was no shade, not even a cloud. I looked around – was anyone nearby? No, they were all asleep in their villas or rousing to the early morning bird songs.

For over an hour I pondered this message and vision, it was a first for me and I wondered whether the vision was the result of my over-imaginative thoughts, or had there been a seed planted in the last few days? On all counts the answer came back that maybe I just needed to accept this and move forward.

Climbing off the wall I looked down and realised that I could have easily rocked forward and fallen many metres into the impenetrable jungle below given that I was in such a state. The time had come for me to act. I knew that I had to share this vision with Lynn.

Lynn is my balance in life; whereas I like to venture into the unknown in every way, from business to leisure, she is the one with her feet on the ground. She brings realism and common sense into our lives. Without her logic, female intuition, expertise and caring ways, I am sure I would have screwed up many times over the previous 18 years that we have been partners.

So here I was in a small villa trying to tell Lynn of my meditation and the strange message I had just received. Our conversation went something like this:

L: "Sweetheart, how was your meditation this morning?"

P: "Just incredible, I received a very strong message" I replied.

L: Cocking an eyebrow at me she asked, "From who?".

44

P: "Er, darling hmmmnn" I mumbled a little and felt like a fool...

L: "What?"

P: Still mumbling, I replied with, "I've just been told to build two Pyramids..."

L: "I don't get you ..."

P: Again I mumbled my response, "... told to build two pyramids here in Ubud".

L. "Did you just say *pyramids*?"

P. "Yes and I saw two of them", I said tentatively.

L. "Peter, we do not even live here, we have retired and we are planning to travel around North America in our Big Rig – *remember*?"

P. Standing on my back foot I replied, "well it was a very strong message".

L. "Okay tell me about it, but honestly, it sounds a bit weird".

So, I sat beside her and explained the whole episode and to her credit she didn't interrupt. At the end, her response was that we should ask Cheryl and Mark what they thought. This was a couple who we knew very well and who were staying with us in Bali at that time.

The end result of that conversation, and a few to follow, was to explore the whole concept and see if it was do-able. After considerable time spent on discussions and research, we all realised it was possibly an awesome opportunity and that all we would need was the land and funding.

Stage 1: The Preparatory Phase

Together with Mark and Lynn, I explored Ubud looking for a possible site, but with no real positive gut feelings. One day Lynn and I had agreed to look at some land being offered, so we went there only to again have that feeling of disappointment. There was nothing special about this rice field. We went for a walk across the road to look at a very small villa sitting on its own. As I neared this villa, I felt a tingling down my spine and the hairs on my arm rising, turning to Lynn she smiled at me and rubbing her own upper arms saying, *"yes I got it too."* Looking at the rice field we were navigating at the time, I wondered whether this could be the place? We carefully made our way down to the far end while trying to avoid slipping off the wet grass into knee-deep mud. By the time we could see the river, we knew this *was the place*!

It took some negotiating to get the land, as the field was not available for purchase or lease, however in the end, the owner did agree to lease it to us. We paid a holding deposit, and he agreed not to replant any rice for the next season, thus giving us time to arrange finance and time for the land to dry out.

The next step was to return to Perth to talk with our friend Chris about raising at least one million Australian dollars for this project that we had roughly estimated to cost between one and two million dollars. Chris is both a good friend and an accomplished financial advisor, but when we told him about our need to find this amount of money to build two pyramids on the island of Bali, he just roared with laughter, while his wife looked on in amazement that we would even suggest such a scheme! Gazing into his glass of red wine he looked at me seriously and said, "Peter, we're in the middle of a global financial crisis." As he swallowed the last of the wine, he started chuckling to himself as he said, "You have started some amazing businesses in the past, but this one is just too far out there for any punters, let alone lending institutions."

So, we took ourselves home wondering what the next step would be, as it all seemed to have been moving in the right direction. Now came the quirky bit that many readers may struggle with.

Not long after we started on our spiritual path, we were introduced to an incredible couple named Jackie and Jim Lindsay who ran 12-week courses over three levels entitled 'Introducing Spiritual Awareness'. These courses were some of the most enlightening times Lynn and I have ever had. Their knowledge, insight, personalities and experience were a tremendous help for us in transitioning from having a business perspective to having a spiritual outlook on life. In the process, we became amazingly close friends. For over ten years they shared their knowledge and provided instruction to many thousands of students, and for free of charge!

During their courses, they introduced us to a special process of communicating with the spirit that they called 'Automatic Writing'. This concept is also known by a number of other names like guided, left hand, or non-dominant hand writing.

It only works if you have a strong belief in your God figure by whatever name it goes by: Spirit, Universe, Krishna, Buddha, Jesus, God, or other. Then you need to put yourself in a meditative state, wrap the white light of protection around you and be prepared to write the answers down that come to you.

Okay, still with me? This is for real from a guy (me) who spent decades in the business world and was previously very skeptical of such suggestions...

This is how it works. You open a book and, on the page next to your dominant writing hand (in both our cases the right side), you write down the question you want to put out there.

Then, reading the question and holding the pen in your non-dominant hand, you start to write down the first word that comes to mind very carefully so you can read it afterwards. Then the next word, and so on, *never* anticipating the next word or sentence. Yes, this indeed works if you follow your heart and are honest with your writings.

So, there we were, Lynn and I each wrote down our question: "God, if you want us to build Pyramids in Bali where is the money?"

After a while Lynn read her answer to me. She had written, "There are people out there waiting to give you the money." I looked at my answer and it was virtually the same as Lynn's. The next question obviously was, *"how do we find them?"*

The answer came through quite cryptically in only four words, "don't spend much money!" I went into a spin, having over forty years in business, how could I raise a million dollars without spending a lot of money on reaching out to investors?

Well, that was the command, so we now planned how to do this. We placed a small classified advertisement in the local newspaper which cost us AUD $40 and we also posted on a free website called 'Gumtree' in Australia, which is similar to Craig's List in North America.

We then surrendered to the Spirit and said, "It is in your hands now. We have followed your directions." Talk about faith! Our faith was now being put to the ultimate test!

There was certainly nothing flash about the advertisements, just a few statements about a business opportunity in Bali and the search for investors. We had a few responses from people asking for the Return on Investment (ROI), however we didn't feel comfortable with these people. We thought that the investors needed to share in our dream and vision, which by this time was very strong.

Within three weeks of placing that message out to the community in Western Australia we raised $750,000 from three investors!

We didn't know them, they didn't know each other, and all of them said, "we're in" before they had even considered the business plan I had prepared. After a 40 minute basic introduction they made up their minds. Now that had to be divine intervention! Were they investing in Peter and Lynn, or the vision, or in Bali, or were they being guided themselves? It was truly the most incredible situation I have ever witnessed, and to this day we, and many others, are in awe of the way it happened.

The most incredible story about the three investors came from Joe and Vicki. On the Saturday Joe, a builder, had taken his son Tommy to the newsagents to buy him an exercise book for his homework and on the way out picked up a newspaper from the counter. When they reached home, Tommy quizzed his dad saying, "Why did you buy the paper, you never even read them?" Joe didn't know the answer. His response was "maybe we have to wrap something in it." Joe and Vicki have strong beliefs and this includes following a vegetarian diet and a very healthy regime and not watching or reading mainstream media.

That afternoon, the newspaper which had been left on the coffee table, rustled gently in the sea breeze blowing through the doors, and when Joe walked past, he glanced down and saw our small ad with the pictures of the Pyramids and text. He called and asked to see us. The next day he stated after just 40 minutes of conversation that he loved the idea and wanted to be a part of it. My initial response was that Joe should take the ideas we had discussed home to his wife Vicki to discuss for her thoughts and input. Joe agreed and left beaming from ear to ear. A few days later, Vicki and Joe both arrived to meet Lynn and me. I fully expected Vicky to apologise for Joe's hasty decision, but that was not how our meeting panned out. After some time chatting, finding out more about us and asking questions about the project, Vicki glanced at Joe who nodded. To our delight he confirmed, "Yes, we're definitely in!"

So, this was the start of our journey to Bali to build the Pyramids of Chi.

Holding to our faith, believing that this project was meant to be, and ignoring the naysayers, we knew our path ahead. Eight months after my message and us realising the vision and challenges ahead, we went to California to sell our beautiful rig and move to Bali, ending our retirement at the age of 64 and surging confidently into a new adventure.

Foot Note

The response from one of our four sons when we said our travels were over and that we were moving to Bali, was this

"Dad you have done some crazy stuff in your life, but we think you have really lost it this time!".

Stage two: Constructing the Pyramids

The challenges began. Anyone who has started a business from scratch knows that nothing is ever as it first seems. At age 29 I had ventured away from organised employment (12 years with the airlines) and believed in my own abilities and desire to create a successful career in start-up businesses. Over the next 36 years, I created a number of excellent businesses and took on several major contracts to do something that many balked at, as there were real doubts about success. With only a few small failures, the rest of my endeavours ensured that my life was full of wonderful accomplishments. Having come from earning a very small income after leaving school with no assistance from my family, I was satisfied with my life in business and the position I then found myself in.

What was missing though was purpose beyond just making money. In 2013, when we made the decision to move out of retirement and carefree travel into this unusual project with the many anticipated stresses and long hours ahead, what drove us was the conviction that we had been chosen for this role. We are not religious but have a strong faith in the Omniscient God.

Nobody could have written the script or even imagined that this could possibly have happened. To this day we often wonder at the path given to us. Looking back over our experiences in life and business, we were certain that we possessed the skills and the tenacity to manage this exciting project.

In a former life, Lynn was an accomplished shopping centre manager. Her position required her to manage the interests of centre owners as well as vendors' needs, to take care of large staff numbers and to monitor accounting issues. Her expertise was good grounding for our new venture.

My background involved starting companies with diverse objects such as satellite communications, a global franchise and a huge marina complex with over 140 staff. These past ventures and a few others, contributed to the skill set that I would need to build such an enterprise in Indonesia.

With the conviction that we could face any challenges, even at retirement age, we threw ourselves into a seven day a week project that took over three years to complete. Dealing with confusing regulations, a culture that so often challenged our own life experiences, and people that put their beliefs and family before work or money had us running in circles regularly.

On top of this, we needed to consider the faith that our team of ten investors had put in us. One of our desires was to see them happy with the end result of the project and to receive a good return on their trusting investment.

Was it an easy process? Never! The long hours, the frustrations with the system, culture, suppliers and staff tested us on a monthly basis. Did it test our own strengths and beliefs in one another? Occasionally, yes. But our deep love for each other overrode any upsets. Would we encourage others to go down the same path? Maybe not at our age, take off 20 years, then for sure!

In early 2017 we completed the development and launched this very different business. We had already captured the interest, sometimes derision and occasionally disbelief in the future of the project from locals and family. During our work on the project, we became used to hearing negative statements, we knew that many of these stemmed from envy or jealousy. We even heard statements of wonderment, that we were undertaking such an incredible experiment on the beautiful island of Bali.

Right from the start, the Universe contributed in the most amazing ways to our growth. We almost destroyed our marketing budget, and exhausted our own funds in the business with cost overruns and unexpected expenses. But each and every day, people came through and our project continued to grow at an incredible rate!

We often examined why these successes were happening when we had such a limited marketing budget, we were soon told in a very direct manner from one of the old hands around Ubud. He believed it was our attitude towards looking after our customers at every level. He ticked off all the obvious ones such as service, ambience, value for money, staff attention, great food and coffee, excellent presentation in the buildings and grounds. Additionally, he explained to us, this project was so different than anything else Bali had to offer. Yep, there were quite a few plus points. The one that we should not have been surprised at, yet he put the highest emphasis on his list of must-dos, was our willingness to mingle, sit with, chat to and become friends with our customers. He said there were probably only two or three other establishments in the region he knew of, where the owners made a point of talking directly to their customers and making them feel personally welcome. He suggested we do a survey of how our customers came to know about us and the Pyramids of Chi. We both felt we already knew, but did the exercise anyway, and discovered in excess of 80 per cent of our visitors were referral or repeats. Having been in business for most of my life, never before had I seen business grow due to such a high incidence of referrals.

We have hundreds of stories and testimonials from people telling us how they ended up at the Pyramids. Despite my years in marketing and Lynn's in management, we both acknowledge that our interactions, and those of our gong players in the Pyramids, played a major part in encouraging our visitors to become our unofficial ambassadors. Word of mouth rules yet again, it just takes one pebble in the pond to start the energies moving.

With an average of ten per cent increase in customers every month and a second year visitor rate of almost 30,000 people where will it reach? So long as we continue to provide something very special for our guests and introduce new products and services, then the future is looking very bright.

With this spreading of the word, Lynn and I are feeling quite accomplished in our developments to date. Today is again Nyepi Day, six years into the dream, and as we write this piece for John's incredible book, we acknowledge that faith and belief in yourself – the guiding force in your life – and a determination to help others, are a winning combination that contribute to our happiness.

It is our desire to see the Pyramids of Chi become the Sound Healing Centre for South East Asia and Australasia, and with the support from the 'ripple effect' of that initial pebble in the pond, we know that this is yet just the beginning of a global expansion, contributing to the happiness of our planet.

In life we are set many challenges, all too often we see people taking the easy road and refusing to face challenges, using many cliched excuses and then probably wondering later "what if?" or "why didn't I?" There are some magical statements about how the crowd is small when you are close to the top of the mountain, or such similar phrases, yet most people in life choose to stop half way up that mountain, or perhaps not even start, because of their own mindset or the influences of others. If in reading our story you are motivated in any way, then we have achieved our desire to see you go that extra mile. In the end it is really about following your heart and not your head.

However, in doing so, please make sure at the same time to help others on that path; do not climb over them or push past them, but encourage and motivate them too. None of us truly knows what drives others and sometimes a small word of encouragement, a word of advice, a pat on the back or even just a good heart-to-heart hug, can achieve incredible results that you may not even be aware of. Don't go seeking returns, instead, know the act of giving is a far greater reward.

At our age, we certainly have been blessed to have this amazing opportunity to introduce Sound Healing to the world with the aid of the powerful energies in a pyramid, the awesome frequencies of the instruments and the visitors to serve. Sometimes perhaps we are being groomed for these opportunities, so we ask all of you to listen to your heart and follow it; we are all being given a chance to affect the big change in consciousness on the planet in our own way – so be vigilant for that opportunity.

Our lives had been mapped out: retirement and traveling; spending precious time with each other and with our sons.

That would bring us happiness in the autumn days of our lives on earth. But when Spirit delivered a profound message to me on that fateful day in 2013, I realised that our search for happiness had to take a different course. By trusting in Spirit, and with the unwavering support of my beloved wife, we have not only harnessed the power of happiness for our own lives, we have helped others find peace and happiness in their lives.

"True happiness is... to enjoy the present, without anxious dependence upon the future."

~ Lucius Anneus Seneca

CHAPTER FOUR

Happiness is a Choice

By Melissa Barkell

The Stage

The stage lights are blinding and the audience is a sea of darkness but they are applauding, cheering for me, and celebrating my journey. My parents, friends, and health community are all out there rooting me on. Five weeks ago, I received the call from my health and wellness company congratulating me on being chosen as one of 15 finalists out of nearly 35,000 participants in our 16-week health transformation challenge. I was not expecting that call, but I am so honored and grateful to represent my company and inspire others to improve their health. Now, here I am, center stage at our New Year Kick Off event, in front of an audience of 6,000 people, and I am filled with love and sincere gratitude. I am so excited to be sharing my story and motivating thousands to transform their lives. It is in this moment that I know that everything that I've gone through — every lesson learned, every experience I've had, every relationship in my life, all of the heartbreak, all of the loss, the good and the bad — has led me to this moment in time and this magnificent opportunity to share my story. I am present, taking it all in and feeling at peace knowing that I am right where I am supposed to be. But my life was not always this way...

The End of My Marriage

My husband and I were together for almost 25 years and married for nearly 12. We had overcome so much as a couple before we were married and throughout our marriage. Together, we raised our beautiful daughter and two Labrador Retrievers. We owned a comfortable home in a quiet, rural neighborhood. We loved each other and I believed that we would be together forever. Although our house was in Montana, my husband worked in New York. We talked on the phone each day and he came home for a few days every couple of months. We led separate lives and eventually, the distance and our lack of communication came between us and impacted our relationship. When my husband decided to end our marriage, my world was shattered. I knew that my husband was not happy in our relationship, but at the time I didn't realize how unhappy I was in our marriage and in other areas of my life. I was going through the motions of life but not really living. My marriage was unraveling and so was my career.

For 11 years, I had been working for an environmental remediation company in the corporate health and safety department. I knew that my job wasn't fulfilling my life's purpose; regardless, I enjoyed working for my supervisor and with my co-workers. My supervisor's passion for his job and my loyalty to him and our team motivated me to continue working there. However, that changed when my supervisor became ill and left the company. Not only did our department get a new supervisor, but there were many changes in our company's leadership. Even though I felt like I was drowning as I went to work each day, I stayed on board for almost three more years. When my divorce was final and we sold our home, I also left that job and career behind. I was struggling in my marriage, at work, and even with my health.

Although I was eating healthy, organic, whole foods most of the time and spending three-four hours a week in the gym lifting weights and doing cardio, I was still 70 pounds overweight, insecure, and I didn't like the way I looked or felt. My knee joints were stiff and ached when I got out of bed in the morning. I lacked energy and didn't like going to the gym, but I made myself go anyway. I was frustrated and couldn't figure out why I couldn't lose weight.

I was miserable, choosing to be unhappy. At the time, I wasn't aware that I have the ability to control my thoughts, feelings, and emotions, and how I perceive the world. I didn't realize that my happiness comes from inside of me and that nothing external will ever bring me true joy. My self-worth was dependent upon the love and acceptance of others. I compared myself to others and worried about what they thought of me (or didn't think of me). I was afraid to get out of my comfort zone because I feared failure. I masked my sadness with fake smiles most of the time.

Even after the divorce papers were filed, I was devastated and didn't want our marriage to end. During the first two months of our divorce, I begged my husband to stay with me, but he wanted the divorce and had already moved on. Depressed and anxious, all I could focus on was losing my marriage and an uncertain future. I felt like a victim and lived in fear. Everything in my life was changing; there was nothing

I could do about it, and I didn't know how I would keep going. I hardly slept but didn't want to get out of bed to face each day. I cried a lot. Every day was a repeat of puffy eyelids and bloodshot eyes.

One day, my friend (and also my personal trainer) called and told me that I had been on her heart, and she asked how I was doing. I hadn't talked with her since before I filed for divorce. (I hadn't shared anything about my pending divorce with anyone outside of my immediate family.) One morning, we met for coffee. I talked. She listened. I told her that I didn't know how I would make it through my divorce if I kept going the way I had been. Then she gave me some pivotal advice: She encouraged me to stop focusing on my husband and what he was doing and to start focusing on myself instead. I told her that I wanted to be happy and feel good about myself. A few years prior, she had introduced me to a superfood nutrition program that I loved and was still using but hadn't been following the whole system. I decided to recommit to my health and wellness and to my nutrition program. I shifted my attention from what I was losing to what I could be gaining, and it was on that day that I made the decision to take my life back.

"We must let go of the life we had planned to have the life that is waiting for us."

~ Joseph Campbell

My Health Transformation

I knew that I needed to accept my divorce and adapt to move forward. I decided to focus on myself and recommit to my health journey. I made positive changes in my nutrition, fitness, and mindset. I was committed to losing weight, feeling good about myself, and being happy. I enrolled in my company's 16-week health and wellness transformation challenge for accountability to myself. I had previously completed this challenge seven times without achieving my weight loss goal. I felt discouraged and defeated each time I submitted my after photos that looked the same as my before photos. During these previous challenges I wasn't really focused on me. I was more centered on taking care of my dogs, my home, and my daughter's and husband's lives. Taking responsibility for my health was not my priority. Even though I was mostly consistent with my nutrition and exercise, I lacked the belief that I could really lose the weight. This challenge would be different because this time I was focused on me and I believed that I could lose the weight.

I fueled my body with my nutrition system and consistently ate healthy. I practiced yoga two-three times per week and started running and hiking. I meditated and journaled to quiet my mind and to discover more about myself. Meditation taught me to be more present in my daily life, to witness and observe my thoughts, feelings, and emotions instead of allowing them to be in control. It taught me to hear my own voice. As I intentionally focused on myself, I began to let go of being a victim and I started a journey of learning to love myself. I became aware that my self-worth and happiness come from within.

I began doing activities that I enjoy and spending time with my family, friends, and my health community, and over the next four months, I was able to release a lot of weight that I had been trying to lose for years. I had more energy and I enjoyed being more active. I was feeling healthier and stronger and was proud of myself! I gained more confidence in my appearance. My clothes were baggy and when I bought new jeans I couldn't believe that had I dropped four sizes! I felt fantastic when my friends, family, co-workers, and health community noticed and shared positive comments.

My Personal Growth Transformation

The love and support of my family and friends is a blessing. My parents, siblings, and best friend are always there to listen with love and support and offer helpful advice. I have many friends who have been there for me and I am so grateful for each of them in my life.

There were so many changes that happened so quickly during our divorce. Both of our dogs passed away. They were an important part of our family, and although they were older (11 and 14); it was still so hard to lose them during this difficult time in my life. We also sold and moved out of our home that we had lived in for 13 years. My daughter and I both struggled with all of the changes and loss that was occurring in our lives. There were some extremely difficult days, but we made it through them together. We are accepting the loss of our old life, overcoming our fears, facing uncertainty, and moving forward. I am grateful that we made it through this challenging season and that we've had one another for support.

My daughter knew how depressed I was during the first couple of months of my divorce and encouraged me to see a counselor. I was struggling with the reality that the future that I wanted to have with my husband was not going to happen. In just a few sessions, my counselor helped me to become aware that even if we had stayed married, the future that I had envisioned with my husband wasn't going to happen. Our communication was broken and we no longer trusted each other.

During my divorce, three friends appeared in my life who taught me some powerful lessons. A new friend reminded me that each day is a gift and that we choose our happiness every day. He wakes up grateful for everyone and everything in his life. He reminded me to not look at my life through the rearview mirror looking back over the past but instead, to focus on the windshield, being grateful for the present and optimistic about the future. The windshield is bigger than the rearview mirror because what happened in the past is not nearly as important as the present and future. I learned that where you are going is more important than where you've been. It's alright not to know exactly what the future holds and it's important to find joy in the journey.

I spent time with an old friend who lives his life without expectations and is content with whatever happens. He doesn't seem to get upset by anything. He chooses not to dwell on problems but instead focuses on solutions. He gives back to his community as a volunteer and goes out of his way to help his friends and neighbors. He surrounds himself with people whom he enjoys spending time with and creates his own happiness by doing activities that bring him joy. He was also going through a divorce and I was impressed by how he still cared for and respected his future ex-wife.

Another new friend taught me to breathe and believe. He invited me to join his tribe and introduced me to so many new friends who inspire me and pour love and belief into me. He encouraged me to let go of my husband with love and to think only loving, positive thoughts about him. He advised me to focus on the good memories with my husband and the positive parts of our relationship and marriage.

The summer after my divorce, I had the opportunity to hear Tony Robbins speak at my company's annual event. He taught us his heart meditation. I learned that my mind and my spirit are connected and must be in alignment to resolve internal conflicts. Through gratitude and learning to trust my heart, I realized that it's possible to overcome my fear of an uncertain future.

That fall, I attended a weekend retreat hosted by my friend in St. George, UT. We read and studied the book, *Wishes Fulfilled: Mastering the Art of Manifesting,* by Wayne W. Dyer on how we are able to create and manifest our wishes. Our imagination is our greatest gift and provides us the unlimited ability to manifest all that we desire.

"When the student is ready, the teachers will appear."
~ Dr. Wayne W. Dyer, *Wishes Fulfilled: Mastering the Art of Manifesting*

My friend and several other powerful trainers spoke about how breathing, meditation, and visualization can help us create better futures. Through sharing our stories and spending time together, I connected and bonded with many new friends.

One trainer read *The Little Soul and The Sun* parable and shared how we are all here to teach each other lessons. After hearing this story, I started to view my divorce as a blessing instead of a burden and began to think of my ex-husband as an angel in disguise. I began to let go of being angry with him and instead chose to feel gratitude for him for having the courage to make a change. He decided to end our marriage because we were both unhappy. He moved on with his life and let me go so that I could become who I am meant to be. Now, I choose only to remember the good times that we had together, to be grateful for the lessons that we taught each other, and to just feel love towards my ex-husband.

Another trainer shared her experience with her own version of the heart meditation. She spoke about how we can turn to gratitude to overcome feelings of sadness, fear, or anxiety. We can thank the Universe for showing us the negative emotion and that we are focusing on that which we do not desire. Then, we can turn our focus toward our desired outcome and with absolute faith; we can believe that what we wish to create will happen.

"If you change the way you look at things, the things you look at change."

~ Dr. Wayne W. Dyer

A personal growth coach spoke at the retreat about some of the reasons that people feel stuck in their lives. He talked about some of the challenges that I was facing like self-judgment, self-worth, and anxiety about the uncertainty of my future. I hired him for group coaching along with some of the new friends that I met at the retreat. Through our six-month group coaching process, my new friends and I created even stronger bonds. One of my biggest takeaways from the coaching sessions was learning that overcoming the adversity that I had been through was so that I could comfort others through similar life experiences. I could be there for those who need someone to listen, understand, and relate to what they are going through. My burdens could be used to bless and serve others.

The following summer, Brendon Burchard was the keynote speaker at my health and wellness company's annual event and shared his personal story about suffering depression and surviving a car accident. At the age of 19, Brendon faced what he felt were life's last questions: "Did I live fully? Did I love openly? Did I make a difference?" His intention to be happy with the answers to those questions led to his own breakthroughs and ultimately to his life's purpose of helping others to live, love, and matter. Hearing Brendon's story helped me realize that we are here to live our lives with passion and purpose, to love and serve others, and to make a positive impact in the world.

Letting Go

One of my mentors invited me to join a book club study group later that summer. We read and studied the book, *Letting Go: The Pathway of Surrender*, by David R. Hawkins M.D. Ph.D. We met once a week in an online video chat to discuss each chapter. This book has had the most significant impact on my personal growth and helped me become aware that I am the source of happiness in my life.

Letting Go describes how to let go of the obstacles to enlightenment and become free from negativity. The mechanism of surrender relieves human suffering and removes the inner blocks to happiness, love, joy, success, health, and, ultimately, enlightenment. Letting go involves being aware of a feeling, letting it come up, staying with it, and letting it run its course without wanting to make it different or do anything about it. Dr. Hawkins believes that a feeling that is not resisted will disappear as the energy behind it dissolves.

In the book, Dr. Hawkins explains that it takes courage and self-honesty to see the negativity and smallness in ourselves. Only when we can acknowledge and accept our own negativity can we possibly surrender and be free of it and rise above it. Peace and happiness are a result of finding our truth within. As we deal with our shadows, we give life to our gifts.

Reading and studying *Letting Go* has been life-changing for me. It has helped me become more aware that my happiness is my choice and that I can choose how I perceive my world and everything in it. I am responsible for creating my reality.

"Life is how you perceive it. The meaning of it is what you project out there. In and of itself, it doesn't mean anything."

~ Dr. David R. Hawkins

There are so many profound concepts that I took away from this book and am applying to my life:

- Know thyself. All of the answers are already within us.

- Attachments are the primary cause of suffering.

- It is not thoughts or facts that are painful but the feelings that come with them. We are not our thoughts. We are not our feelings.

- There is no right or wrong. No one to blame. Not even me. Let go of all judgment and blame of yourself and others. We are all just doing the best we can with what we know.

- Have gratitude for all that is. Have an appreciation for everything and everyone in my life because it has all led me to this point.

- Love is the answer to everything. We are here to give and to be love.

This book helped me become more aware of how I can find more joy in my life by being focused on the present. It does no good to dwell on mistakes or losses from the past, and worrying about the future steals your happiness. All that is happening is right now. Life is about enjoying the journey not the destination.

"It is said that most people spend their lives regretting the past and fearing the future; therefore, they are unable to experience joy in the present."

~ Dr. David R. Hawkins

My Advice

Happiness comes from loving yourself and others. Happiness is a choice. We choose how we perceive everything and everyone. The world is exactly as we perceive it to be.

Having genuine gratitude for everything in your life, be it positive or negative, generates happiness.

Knowing your purpose and having clarity about the future you want to create results in finding happiness.

Transformations are possible in all areas of life. It is possible to evolve into the happy, self-loving, inspired, passionate soul you deserve to be.

As you transform your life, you will change the world! You are infinitely worthy and you deserve to be happy. Have faith in and trust God and the Universe. Trust that you are on the right path and that you are right where you are supposed to be on your journey.

Listen to your heart. Go within. Look inside yourself to find the courage to decide and commit to your own happiness. Overcome your fears with love. You must love yourself first. Love yourself and believe that you deserve to be happy. Let your love for yourself be your levitator. As you discover your happiness, your joy and light will inspire others to find theirs as well. As you find your own happiness, you bring happiness to others.

"We change the world not by what we say or do, but as a consequence of what we have become."

~ Dr. David R. Hawkins

We can determine and create our own happiness. Decide who you are and create the life you want now. Decide what makes you happy. Choose what you want your life to be. Create a vision of your future, imagine it, and bring the feeling with it. Believe and become it.

Be a channel of love light. Take care of, give to, serve, and share with others. Become a being of generosity and service. That which we give flows back to us. Like ripples on the water, every gift returns to the giver.

Prioritize your vibrational feeling each moment. Choose to be in control of your thoughts and emotions. Let go of negative vibrations. Instead of focusing on problems, or negativity, focus on what you want to see and on your future.

My Future

As I stand in the spotlight on this stage, representing and being recognized by my health and wellness company, I am illuminated from the inside out. My journey and my health transformation were not just for me, but for thousands of others who will be inspired by my story to transform their lives. My physical and personal growth transformations have led me to my Divine life purpose and soul mission. It is my mission to inspire and empower others to experience their own life-changing health and wellness transformations, to believe in themselves, to overcome fear with love for themselves and others, and to help them become aware that they choose their happiness and create their future. Knowing my purpose has brought me happiness because now I know that as I love, serve, and give back to others, I feel joy and peace. My health and wellness business is growing. I love sharing my story and coaching others to achieve their own health and wellness goals.

I am grateful for everyone and everything that I've experienced in my life that has brought me to where I am today on my journey. I am genuinely thankful for my health transformation and for my personal growth.

"If you are really thankful, what do you do? You share."

~ W. Clement Stone

"The world is your oyster.
It's up to you to find the pearls."

~ Chris Gardner

CHAPTER FIVE

A GAME

By Konstantin Doepping

Above the entrance is "Ping Pong." Neon tubes flashing colorful, it has a striking resemblance to The Drunken Clam from the television series *Family Guy*. The bar, which regularly supplies beer to the largest idiots, serves as a meeting place. On the other hand, I mostly seek my own company.

Although this establishment is located in the immediate vicinity of my apartment, I have never been here before. I can't say I've ever noticed this pub.

So I go in and hope that redemption from my dull day will be encouraged by entering a new place. As you know, new stimuli lead to new ideas. As I move the proverbial curtain aside, I am surprised to see a cozy room. In the dim warm light, I see a dark wooden counter and sternly lined bar stools. On the back wall, I notice a large mirror running the length of the counter. Soul Asylum's "Runaway Train" plays quietly. Then there is the smell of cigarette smoke, which has become strange to me, reminding me of my childhood. At that time there was no nationwide smoking ban and wherever I went to eat with my parents, people would be smoking cigarettes while dining.

Normally, I avoid pubs where smoking is permitted despite the ban. Since I have no balcony, it is virtually impossible for me to rid my clothes of the stench overnight. Besides the consequences of alcohol, I'll take another souvenir home today.

In order to be able to retreat into my thoughts, I sit down on the short side of the counter. From here it is possible for me to survey the space and to get an idea of society. I share the bar with a dozen other characters who have come alone as well. The exception is two couples sitting at a table by the window and obviously having fun. They talk to a guy who stands beside their table and appreciates their exuberant cheerfulness. I ignore them and concentrate on quenching my thirst.

"White or red?" Asks the waitress over the counter.

Although I think of beer, my answer is, "Red."

The waitress is wearing a high black braid, baring her gray hair at the base. Her facial lines tell of long years as a barmaid, service force and therapist for countless guests. She is a classic gastronomy pearl - warm and straightforward.

She reaches behind her and grabs from a collection of open wine bottles that looks like meerkats and pours me a glass. I also get a bowl of salted peanuts next to the glass of wine. This is generally the case of a sleight of hand of gastronomy, but I could never agree with the assumption. If I sit in a bar and drink, it is certainly not because I push half a kilo of salted peanuts into my mouth.

"The wine makes you look better," she says without looking at me.

German as I am, I want to reply with "What a cheek!" But I let it stay. I've already bitched enough about the weather today.

I alleviate my horror with the thought that probably every cowboy who enters a bar like this on his own is looking for some salvation. And she is actually right about it, even if I'm not as lonely as the rest here. I live with my girlfriend, but today I let her sit alone at home. I cannot seem to form a clear idea of what my problem really is, nor do I feel like talking about it. This is actually stupid of me, because my girlfriend's mere presence has often been helpful to get rid of heavy thoughts. Today, however, I decide for a Hollywood-like a visit to a bar.

If you cannot identify your problems, it's probably because there are several things that bother you. Privacy, job, goals and expectations, and anyway, everything else that happens around us. That's how I explain it. Add to that this unnatural world of concrete, plate, and dog shit that separates us from ourselves.

A Big City Trauma.

I take a sip and cannot remember the taste a second later. So I wave my hand over the glass and take another sip and try to focus on the wine. I hope nobody just watched me.

Back to the hiccups. In trying to analyze each point individually, I lose myself in the quicksand of thoughts. The more one deals with them, the worse they become. Like I said, sometimes everything is just too much. You want to do everything right and always plan the next step. But is that possible, and is the will to achieve that not already pre-programmed evil? I often compare myself to people

77

of a different generation without ever having spoken to a 19th-century person. They had a hard life. Romantic hard. The worries lay in securing their existence and bringing the family through. And me? I strive for self-realization, reputation, and financial success. A tragic game of mutually-related problems. To escape from the mental chaos, I tune it off with a "bullshit!" Besides, the people living in the old empire were poor suckers, too.

I look around again. The Association of Sprung Couples is just about to leave. After putting on their jackets, they disappear laughing through the door. From the other end of the room, I hear the annoying *tok-tok, tok-tok* of a table tennis ball. Oh, yes, the bar is called Ping Pong.

Glass of wine number one is done. The waitress looks over and waits for a sign from me. I nod and she fills my glass.

When depressed, you question everything. An escaped thought opens up. Distractions offer themselves like advertising of discounted offers. Sometimes even a change of location satisfies.

"Hey!" a voice calls into the room.

I look uninvolved at my glass.

"Do you want to challenge me?"

This time I raise my head and see the guy who was talking to the couple earlier. He's standing at the end of the counter and looks at me with a big smile on his face. Since I don't quite understand whether he means me, I point questioningly at myself. Leaning against the counter, he holds a table tennis bat in my direction and makes an affirmative gesture.

"Thank you," I say and wave him off. I contrive a smile. The feeling of displeasure rising in me confirms my negative attitude. "Don't get on my nerves!" I think.

At that moment, the guy makes his way to me and is quickly standing to my left.

"You are afraid of losing, huh?" he says, nudging me with the bat.

"Yes, probably!" I reply, hoping to get rid of the guy.

Unpleasant

"Do you see this dude back there?" he asks me loudly. "He had no chance against me. Can you do it better?"

His pronunciation is clearly underlined by an Italian accent. He is in his mid-40s. I can smell cologne. His hairstyle reminds me a lot of Roberto Baggio. Brown curls are divided by a blue headband into top and bottom. That doesn't look good. Certainly not for me, because it is clear that he would be persistent.

He's about half a meter away from me, and I'm watching his gray stubble.

"Find another victim. I'm not social today," I say.

"No, no, I'll ask you!" he replies and places a racket in front of me on the counter. He makes an inviting movement and walks to the back area where the table tennis table is.

My approach has always been to take life with both hands. Now I see how far I am from it. The constructed image of self-pity and self-therapy confronts me.

I look at the waitress with raised eyebrows. She had made no move to keep our conversation private as she was listening across the counter. She smiles tenderheartedly and makes a head movement in the direction of the table tennis table. I feel edgy.

"All right, then. Things cannot get worse." I sigh to myself and make my way over to the table. I take the wine glass with me and look at my opponent more closely. He not only wears this headband, he has a light blue sports jacket on. Embroidered on the back: "Table Tennis Tony." I laugh. What the hell is that guy? I think I got off at the wrong station.

The glass, my lifeline, I put on a stool near the table tennis table. The speakers now sing "Broken Wings" by Mr. Mister.

"We play until eleven. Best of three!" He calls over the plate. "I'm starting."

0:1

0:2

0:3

He laughs happily.

0:4

0:5

Jubilation.

0:6

0:7

He looks over at me in disbelief.

0:8

0:9

Silence.

0:10

0:11

"Poor!" Table Tennis Tony throws over to me and seems to have no guilty conscience. I'm less disturbed by my embarrassment than by his irritating behavior. If my emotional world was depressing at the beginning of the bar visit, the guy is just putting me in a state of shame. "What's this? You play without soul!" My face goes as red as a beetroot.

"I am doing you a favor! You wanted to play, I played with you. What's up with that?" I stammer defiantly at Table Tennis Tony. I feel caught. Ridiculous. When you are stuck in the underground car park of emotions, the ego becomes very strong and determines how you think and act.

"Should I give you a hug?" he replies, gesturing the Italian way. "You played like a little baby. Talk to your wine and pity yourself. That's why you're here, aren't you?"

Welcome to Napoli

I like to cultivate non-violent communication. Everyone has his say; no one is the victim of verbal attacks. And in the end, there is the hope of peaceful coexistence. Meanwhile, I have deleted freak-outs from the repertoire. Add to this the desire to live mindfully. Prudence always before ecstasy.

What a Blindness ...

Seeking an answer, I look around the bar. The music is playing. At the other end of the table, my opponent is just as motionless.

He was right, but a verbal confession on my part is too much to ask. As I played, neither he nor I could have been satisfied with it. Why should one get involved in a game with someone who shows no commitment? My face tries to smile away from the situation. Such a smile out of embarrassment, out of defense. I hate it because at that moment you give up control. Since I cannot think of anything better, I shrug.

"I love to get a perfect punch," says Table Tennis Tony, blasting the uncomfortable situation very elegantly. "Boom! The ball leaves the racket splendidly."

He shows me several times, in a kind of dry run, what a forehand has to look like. Just that one that gave me an embarrassing defeat. The bat in his right keeps swinging in the air. Table Tennis Tony is slightly crouched.

"Why am I so much better than you?" he asks me. Yes, I've already learned that he was straightforward.

"You play regularly, and your racket probably costs more than your jacket," I reply, chuckling at the outfit.

"Nope! You take yourself too seriously and don't enjoy the game. That's shit. It's all up here." He taps his forehead with the bat. "The racket is a standard model. Like the one you hold in your hand."

Of course, I know what is important in table tennis, golf, or other sports. Often one reads of sports psychologists who are hired by professionals to tame their own minds. Will you

82

ever win this fight? In any case, that always sounds like a lot of work to me.

"You need to know where you are good at and how to apply it to the game. Forehand or backhand? One thing you will be able to do better. No matter. If we both bring our strengths, our relationship will be better."

Masterclass

Now he shows me his backhand. A movement that starts in front of the chest and leads the bat towards the table. I can clearly see beads of sweat on his nose.

"Open your heart. So you can remember it. A nice mnemonic, right? I love it, and it works," he explains with a grin. He is obviously pleased to give a talk about it. He's a man in his element.

Before I realize it, we are playing a few balls back and forth without counting points. I try the forehand, want to create the topspin, want to hit the sweet spot. "First of all, you are holding the racket wrong." The ball flies from side to side, over the net, and sometimes through the room. "Relax your hand and swing until the end."

Then I am "opening my heart" and I hit a backhand. When the ball rushes to the other side at high speed, he reacts with a "very good!" We play the same sport as we did minutes before, but negativity and disinterest turn into positivity and activity.

Meanwhile, the inner vibrations have noticeably smoothed. The funny guy actually gets me out of my misery. Undoubtedly not very carefully, at least according to my standards, but cordially and successfully. He went after me as I hung there at the counter like a rag on the balcony railing. Now I begin to think there is something more benevolent about him. I must have looked pitiful. He wanted to help me. Fine, peculiar Table Tennis Tony.

"The bat is the most important thing. Be good with it and understand that it is the link to the game. But don't be fooled. A racket that looks expensive does not mean better play," he explains, looking at the piece of wood he holds in his hand. "The pleasure of shiny things is a short one. Learn how to deal with it. Play with soul and seriousness. Only then we both have something of it."

I feel the weight of the bat in my hand and touch the wooden surface. A PlayStation controller definitely has less charm. There is no human touch at the end of it, no sense of communion.

Tok-tok, Tok-tok

And then there is this unique sound, a sound produced by the celluloid ball. As the ball hits the surface, the sound is determined by the rhythm. Heartbeats of a game. Our ears are the ECG. We can perceive what speed is being played. Dropouts are breaks and mistakes are always chances for new beginnings. The playlist is framed in the beginning and end. We open our hearts.

It's about time for another round of victory and defeat. My hope for success has increased only insignificantly, but it feels right now. Because even as a loser you can benefit. The poisoned thoughts seem to have vanished. In addition, I make an acquaintance for an evening, maybe longer.

Again and again, I remember the words I read in one of the Dalai Lama's books: "There are no strangers, only friends whom one has not met." I love this sentence, it makes life a lot easier.

And then there's the game itself: a small journey with an unknown destination—a task that gives me responsibility for myself and at the same time for my opponent. I have my fate in my own hands, but at the same time, I am dependent on my counterpart. We are nothing without each other. Is this possible with a game one plays alone? I do not think so, and I'm sure it is the same for Table Tennis Tony. He could have spent this night alone at home, as he may have during many past nights. Is he in a relationship? Irrelevant. The role he plays here is of tremendous value. For me, for him, and as I have already noticed earlier in the evening, also for others. He feels joy in what he does and lets us all participate. This is a gift that I am certain will benefit me from this evening on, and I've gained a mindset that I will take with me.

Second Chance

Since I lost the first game, I can start the next. I concentrate on my forehand. I enjoy swerve balls. However, I lose the game. Of course, I lose; of course, I would prefer to score 11 points first. Nothing is better than success. But in the end, I make five and get the respect and gratitude of my opponent. We shake hands like real sportsmen. Both players won today.

I leave the bar and stop for a moment. The fresh night air is good. I grin from cheek to cheek and hope nobody just watched me.

"Happiness isn't the absence of problems; it's the ability to deal with them."

~ Steve Maraboli

CHAPTER SIX

Happiness

By Ritu Bali

From time immemorial, life celebrates itself in simple yet joyous occasions – Beginning with the baby shower, new parents enjoy each milestone of their child's growing years, marriages, celebrations and birthdays, the list is endless. These moments encourage us to live up to our highest potential and later become happy memories which are cherished forever. These memories become more precious and are re-used as stress-busters for pleasant relief. These memories are welcomed wholeheartedly, time and again - as it is a human tendency to seek happiness, and there is nothing wrong with it - provided one consciously attempts to bring such moments back to the present so that the goal of happiness is achieved. Happiness is a state of mind, often self-controlled. It is a sentiment or a feeling that uplifts the mood and reinforces a positive attitude, behavior and action. The aim of life should be to attain happiness and to spread it. "Happiness held is the seed; happiness shared is the flower " - author unknown. George Santayana, the author of *The Life of Reason* also supports this by saying: "Happiness is the only sanction in life; where happiness fails, existence remains a mad lamentable experiment."

Happiness is when life has fulfilled its need. This contentment or sense of fulfillment gives immense pleasure. There are numerous kinds of happiness that spring from innumerable sources. Broadly speaking, there is an instant - or 'momentary happiness' - which is achieved from material gains fulfilled after hard labor. In other words, the achievement of material goals gives a certain relief. This relief has a magical feeling but is short-lived and fades with time. The expectation of greater results again reinforces the strain to perform better and too toil for excellence. The contentment gained from purchasing gold, diamonds, expensive cars or bungalows does not stay for long. The mind soon desires something better, and as time passes, the joy of possessing them gradually fades. Evidently, materialistic happiness only provides momentary relief. Though momentary or material happiness is short-lived, there is no harm in reaching this type of bliss. Material happiness supports our finances, needs and aspirations. These aspirations motivate us to perform better, to yield the desired result.

Moving on from material happiness one could reach the second level of happiness which could be termed as gratification attained from 'giving' and 'gratitude.' This comes from acts of kindness, character, giving back to society and with feelings of gratitude for what the Almighty has bestowed as blessings. This kind of inner solace is unmatchable as it comes from strings of faith. Discarding our false ego and making sacrifices for the benefit of society; these are completely 'human' traits that make us distinct from animals. The act of giving and being beneficial to others brings self-worth and great feelings of unmatchable satisfaction. *The Bhagwad Gita* says: "False ego is the most subtle feature of the inferior, material energy. It's the very point of contact between spirit and matter......False ego is what makes us think that our 'self' and our external body are the same. The reality is that we all are spiritual". This means that one could rise from the material happiness to spiritual by curbing the demon of false ego leading to inner peace and tranquility. *Shiva Puran*, the Hindu scripture, says "Your ego is the only thing that prevents you from attaining greatness. It is your ego that comes between your goals and your dreams, and makes you a less loving person". My take on the above statement is that material happiness is only a means and not an end.

Beyond material happiness, above even the satisfaction that comes from helping others, there is, as I experience it - a third kind of bliss, which is trapped within us. This elated state is found in meditation, through constant practice and self-restraint. Though challenging to put in words, this is the ultimate state of relaxation and "self- realization." Additionally, the reading and understanding of scriptures, spiritually connecting with the soul, harmonizing oneself with the cosmos and the over-soul, resonating with the waves of existence and practicing ethics in real life brings genuine peace, solace and happiness. This solace stays forever and cannot fade with time.

This kind of joy is beyond description and can be reached by the few who toil for it. This state of extreme joy is a transition from the material to the spiritual state of understanding. It is above the 'thingness' of things, from actions, emotions, attachments, worldly desire and expectations." In this state, a person rises above the animal state of discontentment that stems from personal woes, worries, anger, lust, attachments and greed. I am a learner who is trying to understand this state for sure as an observer from life. There were moments in a complete 'trance' when I felt this kind of extreme joy. Reinforcing one's ethics and spirituality brings about a complete change of outlook on the world.

I strongly feel that life gives ample opportunities and experiences to learn and grow from happenings around us. One has to steal moments of happiness by cultivating poise within. In the journey of life, there have been many happy moments that I now recollect like gems and feel blessed. The excitement of getting my new job as a postgraduate teacher at the age of twenty three, the contentment of completing my quest for a philosophy degree in English literature in a record period of 18 months, getting married to my soul mate, being blessed with a lovely family, my success as a writer of poetry and prose, my book revealing events and many other such moments give me intense joy and gratification of attaining my goals.

These moments were blessings from above but even these moments cannot be mistaken for permanent moments of eternal bliss. My true elated cherished moments were not from personal gains but by giving back to society. This began a bit earlier in my life as my dad encouraged me to raise donations for the blind and for the old aged homes. At the tender age of seven, I realized the joy of giving which continues till this day. I joined the theosophical society of Agra and learned the importance of purposeful coexistence with empathy for the have nots.

Remember, no one can rob you of your happiness except you. Happiness comes in small packages and gestures which can be just a loving hug, compassion, gratitude, care, a sense of belonging, a pat on the shoulder, a gentle kiss, even a cup of coffee to bring a smile back to someone's face. It could be as simple as quality time spent with grandparents, parents, kids, society - anyone who needs some love. Spreading love and care gives a beautiful sense of fulfillment that money cannot buy.

Pain is not absent when one talks of a happy state. One has to stop deriving pleasure from the pain of the past. Ignoring the sad memories of the muck of the past is the best strategy to survive. The subjective state of well-being can denote a happy state from life's imperfections. Learning from imperfections, accepting the flaws and moving on in life with purpose gives a sense of control. "To live happily is an inward power of the soul" – Marcus Aurelius, Meditations. A gratified state can be achieved by keeping excess emotions at bay and by maintaining balance in the high and low tides of life. *The Shiva Puran* mentions: "Shiva is called 'Neelkanth' as he swallowed poison named 'halahala' that emerged from the ocean. This symbolizes that one should take negativity in its stride and remain positive."

Celebrating each baby step, each milestone of life, bringing positive changes in self and society gives unmatched gratification. During my teaching tenure as a postgraduate teacher in Kota, India, I devoted my evening time to teaching less fortunate students - mostly poor - who needed extra attention as they were weak in their studies. I tried to explain concepts to them and bought them their books. Giving them tutorials developed a special bond between these kids and me. I received an abundance of love and respect from them and seeing them prosper gave me delight. With this simple gesture, I learned that there was so much to give back to society and to make this earth a happy planet.

When we discuss different kinds of happiness, we should realize that these are not in conflict or affinity with each other. Material happiness, spiritual happiness, happiness achieved through generosity in varying kinds and is of equal importance. For instance, one has to work and deliver to reach the goals of material happiness. A financially stable person is best suited to help others. It is not debatable; however, that one should maintain the balance between need, greed and obsession. Worldly needs can be endless. Sometimes a person reaches his goals and yet remains unhappy. Finding the balance between our needs and greed brings inner solace. Sharing and helping selflessly gives eternal joy.

Aristotle divided the state of happiness into four major types:

Level one is 'Laetus' which is happiness derived from material objects.

Level two is 'Felix' which means through 'ego gratification' by accomplishing targets and goals of life.

Level three happiness is 'Beautitudo' this state is derived by doing good for others by making the world a better place. This is the source of permanent bliss.

The final state of happiness is called 'Sublime Beautitudo.' This kind of contentment is attained by spirituality and ethics and by practicing the above three levels as well and also by maintaining the right balance between them.

"Happiness is the meaning and purpose of life, the whole aim and end of human existence."

- Aristotle.

People mostly reach the' Laetus' and 'Felix' levels of happiness by accomplishing their goals. However, the gratification acquired from these levels is short lived as people start working towards further goals.

By reaching level three 'Beautitudo' one can make success purposeful by helping others. The former two levels are worth working for if it is not for a selfish consumption for "ego gratification." One should try to practice ethics in a life span to reach the final state of happiness which is by attaining the fourth level as explained by Aristotle. Laetus, Beautitudo and Felix should work in coherence to reach the 'sublime beautitudo' or 'final state' of happiness. This could also be called as an elated state of attaining and understanding spirituality. This definition explains the meaningfulness of life to a fruitful existence.

Let us take, for instance, an example from Mother Nature. Nothing in nature lives for itself. The trees do not eat their fruits, the flowers do not smell their fragrance, and neither do the rivers drink their water. The sun illuminates and the moon brightens the night. Nature teaches us to illuminate and it spreads fragrance and fruitfulness in the life of others.

Happiness occurs by training the mind constantly to perceive goodness in everything. Positivity is a personal choice which no one can constrain. The quality of one's thoughts is one's responsibility and that decides the state of happiness or unhappiness which one develops. A house becomes a 'home' when a family lives with love, laughter and a sense of belonging. Laughter indicates happiness and is therapy like good music. A happy home makes a happy society and a progressive nation. "Weeping may endure for a night, but joy cometh in the morning"- Bible Psalms 30:5.

Happiness cannot be attained until the mind is at rest. It breathes and breeds within. Most people depend on their happiness from others and feel dejected when deceived. Expectations of happiness are a cause of sorrow. True joy does not wait for the right moment. It comes from within, from the deeds well done for self and others, acts of courage, honesty and gratitude that bring value to the society. Every day is a blessed new day of newer opportunity to thank the Lord and to start anew. Each day is an opportunity to find and spread cheer through the stretch of twenty-four hours that could change sadness to a smile on someone's face.

There may be many reasons to find conflict, but it only takes a few moments to uplift the heart with joy. This joy is trapped within us and the more one shares it, the more it spreads like an infectious disease. For this, one has to learn to erase all negative memories of the past from the mind. Also, one has to accept the imperfections of life. Nothing can be frozen into permanence forever. Life should be taken into totality with its ups and downs and happiness should be made a priority.

Happiness is a conscious choice. Its value runs deep and effects impacts life and also the attitude towards life and its perspectives. A cynical person would always find fault with everything. These negative emotions suck away the juice of life and make it dry and dull. Did you know one can rewire the brain to be happy by merely recalling those moments and memories that one is grateful for? This does not mean that the 'struggle' was absent while achieving these past accomplishments. It is good to remember the best part and gather energy from it to better oneself. Whenever I remember my struggles of getting a job, my troubles in pregnancy that arose because I am diabetic or the difficulties of staying away from home while at work. I recall the times I fulfilled my duties as a teacher, how blessed I am to be a mother of two beautiful children, and how lucky I was that

I completed my research in the record time of eighteen months. Despite all these odds I was married to a caring man who became my life. These blessings are always abundant compared to more than the troubles I underwent and filled me with magical moments of bliss of which no one can rob me.

Life is always rife with events and incidents. The moments that bring cheer, hope and survival are best to be rewired in the mindscape. These moments make the heart light and help to ward away dark thoughts and are a source of inspiration during difficult times. Pursuing hobbies such as painting, music, art, sculpture, and literature all bring solace. It is cathartic and stays forever. I started painting and writing poetry from my twenties, my work published in well-known literary magazines, my art featured in numerous exhibitions. These hobbies gave me the inner joy of self-worth. Creating art is like finding a treasure of which one is proud of forever. It is not wrong to say that 'a work of art is a joy forever.'

"Our happiness depends on wisdom all the way."

- Sophocles, Antigone.

Positive reinforcement is a continual process and comes from daily practice. Negative forces try to pull us down. Ignoring trivial happenings takes skill, perseverance, patience and mind control to deal with it. Severe problems of life need a positive approach. That is why hobbies help to give vent to mind and uplift the mood. The happiness gained from this cathartic process cannot be bought with money.

Feeling 'better' or 'bitter' is a very personal choice. One cannot motivate a person to be very happy unless there is a will to surrender continuously. Every problem has a solution. There is a need to find the right key to unlock life's uncertainties. Each moment is worth living and that too wholeheartedly. Difficulties, problems, crisis, and pain, are an integral part of the life journey. Let us accept them gracefully. Unnecessary comparisons, judgments, biased notions can be avoided for a peaceful mind at rest. *The Shiva Puran* says: "An uncontrolled mind can lead you to live a disastrous life. You cannot win battles when you lose focus and fall prey to your desires and addictions. Therefore, it's necessary to keep your mind aligned with your goals and heart too." Emotional baggage from the past should be dropped off as it eats away one's sanity and sound judgment. Precious years of life should not be wasted in conflict. Acceptance and sustenance to the will of the Almighty is the key to happiness. Count your blessings rather than your curses and misfortunes. Mistakes make us human and need to be mended without embarrassment. Life should be made lighter like the waves that never stop moving in the ocean. One has to accept life as it is, to be happy.

Working for opportunities that give happiness is a good idea but scrambling for things/goals, cursing others, finding faults kill the golden moments of life leading to feelings of frustration and despair. The rainbow sparkles in the sky from a single raindrop to cheer countless souls. The human tendency of fault finding robs life of its rainbow. 'Perfection' is not present in reality but positive attitude fetches many moments of tranquility.

"It is neither wealth nor splendor but tranquility and occupation which gives happiness."

- Thomas Jefferson, letter to Mrs. A.S.Marks (1788).

In the journey of life, there were moments when I completely broke down. This happened especially when I conceived despite my diabetes after two spontaneous miscarriages. The fear of losing this pregnancy weighed heavily on my mind despite visiting the clinic regularly for checkups. Congenital disabilities and complications are common in such cases - and hence-concerned women in the clinic with lean, sad or stressed faces worried me about my child's health. My prayers for my baby were answered. She came hale and hearty into this world. The frequent insulin injections and pain from other medications was nothing before the joy of hearing the first wail of my baby after my caesarian section.

Life is never a smooth sail. The onus is on us whether to proceed with lighter steps or with a heavy heart. "One is never as fortunate or as unfortunate as one imagines" - LA Roche. The sense of fulfillment is acquired after one finds a victory in the battle. However, one should never forget to share one's success and happy moments with those who are less fortunate. Sharing happiness doubles the delight. Helping others find happiness brings contentment of worth which can be achieved along with personal goals. It would be somewhat selfish to celebrate for oneself. Human life should rise above these animal instincts.

These happy moments should be shared; sad times should be accepted gracefully. In losing a battle, poise should be maintained, to take it as the will of God. Moving on with the tides is life and makes it worth living.

I am in my late forties - in the middle of life, perhaps. From the experiences that life has given, I can infer a lot more understanding with maturity. By earning for myself, I feel contented to be able to provide help to others who are less fortunate. Reading and re-reading of scriptures gives me intense strength, contentment and peace. It is a regular feature now and I wish to understand the occult more closely. Another thing that lifts my mood is the world of poetry and art.

Poetry and art are magical therapies for my soul, and I wish to pursue them to the end. With this mindset, I want to spread positivity and strength with my articles that could bring healing, happiness and peace to people who need the reassurance of their inner strength. I am already working on myself and trying to better myself daily by practicing affirmative action, speech and thought. These baby steps of finding bliss have started from home; from family, friends and acquaintances on to larger groups. So, by changing myself, I am bringing a change in my life and for those around me for good - and better yet, for excellence; from now and into the near future.

I have clearly understood that happiness comes from small packets of trust, forgiveness, and cheer and by shedding anger. Hearty laughter re-energizes me with the feeling of being 'alive.' These moments mean much more to me than the luxuries money can buy. I have resolved to be a giver of love and happiness rather than a beggar of happiness reaped through expectations. I have conditioned my mind to ignore the irrelevant and to be more purposeful to keep at peace. So let us energize ourselves and seek happiness within as there are loads and loads of it within us. As you know " The joyfulness of a man prolongeth his days"- Ibid 30:22. My aspirations to achieve inner happiness for the future are not very big, though they are essential. I think of living a fulfilling life and a meaningful one too so that when I look back in time, I feel proud.

I am striving presently and working not only towards my personal goals but also practicing habits that would bring about refinement, sound judgment, and progress in my approach. I have learned to conquer my fears and inhibitions and ward them off from time to time, as these random thoughts destroy progress, knowledge, goals, and happiness. "Everybody loves a kidder; but nobody lends him money" - Arthur Miller, *Death of a Salesman*. So, it is essential to be self-sufficient to be happy and to help others. In my personal goals towards gratification, I want to explore the world by traveling so I can experience people and culture intimately. I love meeting people. Besides providing a better life for my family, engaging myself in my vocations of poetry, painting and writing articles, I want to read more scriptures as they bring me intense thoughtfulness and inner peace. These goals keep me inspired and give me direction.

I want to unlock my brain to achieve my goals so that I may be capable enough to help bring changes for good in my family and society. Charity begins at home and I have been raised with this value. These goals make me enthusiastic and I may not end up like many people who are always confused to find the door to happiness. I am working to make each moment of life a priority by focusing on goals for the future.

The brightness of the light guides us to reach the door to the completion of goals; the steep terrain and perspiration adds meaning to the purpose of existence and makes the journey fruitful. Every moment lived happily is a life worth living. Make happiness a habit by default - and it will stay forever. It gives me solace when I write articles inspired by *The Bhagwad Gita*, *The Shiva Puran* and *Upanishads*. They help me write about positivity, inner strength, ethics, integrity and values. Shiva was called 'maha yogi' or a great meditator because he mediated for the wellbeing of the universe. "You can win half the battle just by being calm in a stressful situation. It is the best strategy for sorting out a problem"- *The Shiva Puran*.

Connecting with people and helping them find their power gives me contentment that I am spreading the light. It is evident that mental health is a way to bring physical wellness and therefore achieve the goal of happiness in life. In modern times the best way to help others is to make them realize that mental strength can be gained through positive thoughts. Life becomes worth it when it is made useful. Sharing and caring is what brings the moments that remain cherished. To announce one's acts of kindness does not sound good, but I would continue my social service for the needy as an integral part of my life and make it a mission to be pursued. I am associated with such people and will keep on spreading these vibrations of love and kindness.

Living without expectations from others is like living free. I have made it a habit to not depend on people or circumstances for my golden moments. Scriptures bring me the calm and control of mind to see the brighter side of everything. A controlled mind full of gratitude and a mission to find a smile on the faces of others is a beautiful idea.

Here my search for happiness ends. I have discovered its bountiful reward trapped within. A heart full of love keeps it safe and protected. I hope these experiences and thoughts bring my reader's benefit and bring this isolated continent to discovery. Yes, the discovery of happiness itself is the sole meaning of existence.

"For every minute you are angry you lose sixty seconds of happiness."

~ Ralph Waldo Emerson

CHAPTER SEVEN

THE LITTLE BIRD
A STORY OF HOPE

By Heather M. Bleakman

It is a rainy Monday, so I don't bother with my hair other than sweeping it into a side bun. She was barely sixteen, so I pull a few pieces free, trying to give it a messier look to inwardly defy this ancient tradition of loss. There is something about the rules of it all that has me feeling caged. As we walk closer to the front of the building, I see this looming dark thing, pretentious in its customary right, pull around the corner and up under the awning. I think about what is inside, and I stop dead in my tracks, the rain from our umbrella dripping uncomfortably down the back of my legs.

"Let's go back to the car," I beg, before I know the words have truly escaped my mouth. "We don't have to go inside if you are not ready," my wife answers. Then, in that moment, as if being summoned, a grieving mother gracefully steps out of the hearse and I reverently bow my head. With her head tilted just slightly down, she instinctively reaches out to feel the young arm of her one remaining daughter, tangible beneath the warmth of her skin. "I would hold onto her, too," I realize. "My mother held onto me."

I take in the young girl's pressed black dress, little black pumps, and smooth hair with the smallest braid laid in place to keep her hair neatly out of her eyes. I wonder if all of this soothes her heart, or if her heart, like mine, is beating wildly in spite of the forced order. "You are getting ready to bury your dead," I weigh the thought. "How can this feel right?"

I had refused to wear black, when it was me. I refused the neatness of formal ceremonies, of great cars that are crafted to carry rotting bodies, and of churches with printed follow-along instructions of rehearsed speeches, tidy grief, and lament hymns. I refused certain things even as my mother begged. This crushed my heart. And, still, it was his only request. It was the one promise I could still keep to him. I can't help but wonder if I made the right choice to keep the promises to my departed brother over the wishes of my very present mother. Maybe my mother reached for the wrong arm. The mother standing before me now is lucky to have this daughter, willing, even, to offer compliance with the great thief for the greater good of the living.

I feel her gaze on me and know I should look up. I should look into her eyes. I should put my arms around her saying, "I understand," but instead I cower from the enormity of what is happening to this family. I feel the familiar ache of grief clawing its way up my throat, and I dread being eaten alive by it. Then, I command myself, "Take one deep breath." Before I exhale, a silent prayer moves through my spirit as I walk from underneath the cover of the umbrella and into the gray morning of the weeping clouds. I exhale and start moving forward again. I move away from this holy place and head towards the church; I am alone, ashamed, cold, and wet.

I feel hundreds of crying souls all around me. I look to the front of the sanctuary and count towards the back. Fourteen. There are fourteen pews in one row; there are four rows on the lower level, and, after you climb to the top of the rounded stairway, there are just as many above. They are full. All of them.

I look at the nearest pew and count to twelve. Twelve people. Some pews have a few more, some a few less. That means there are approximately one thousand, three hundred and forty-four warm bodies surrounding me. I stop my nervous adding, and I look for the newly polished wood that holds the one body we all wish was warm.

I wonder if the room will flood in so much sadness, and then I look down at the hardwood floors and see large puddles forming around each breathing body, every second growing in mass until they form one large pool. Drowning is one of my great fears, and I don't see any life vests attached to the end of the pews. My chest feels heavy and I unwillingly add to the forming ocean around me and imagine a great ship being compromised from the inside. I imagine this sadness drowning us all.

Then, a gentle hand wraps around mine and encourages me to the nearest seat on the very last row. I move close to her and feel the safety of her leg against mine. I try to stay still, but the frantic tapping of my foot has a life of its own. I feel her hand quietly rest on my moving knee, and I absorb her calmness like a famished child who hasn't eaten in days.

I look behind me to see how many paces it will take to get to the door that will allow my escape, and its nearness gives me a small amount of courage, so I direct my attention back to the empty podium. She whispers, "I am right here with you." There in my spouse's eyes I find the small, kind smile I wanted to give the mother outside. Without thinking twice, she tangles her fingers with mine and begins the slow dance of her thumb along the outer edge of my hand.

It is time to look forward to the front of the chapel and watch a life flash across a projector. It takes just seven minutes to watch all of her. Seven minutes and sixteen seconds.

I listen to her mother relive stories while her father wordlessly grieves. I feel her 13-year-old sister stand tall with the strength of a saint as she bares part of her soul. I watch her best friend fall to the floor and then sob as she is carried out, and I anger at the persistence of the selfish woman in front of me who is making a spectacle out of her own daughter's grief as she wails and pulls her child in uncomfortably tight. This woman's red lipstick bleeds painfully into the creases of her lips as she looks around to see who is watching, and I am terrorized as she reminds me of someone in a horror film.

My mouth opens to scream as I feel the water rising up around me. This will be the last breath before my head is submerged. I gasp until my lungs are full, and then the room suspends nearly motionless like a sunken vessel, me with it.

The last time I felt the cover of depression, I was not much older than the teenager we are here to mourn. I remember feeling the great weight of gut-wrenching pain and being too weak to hold it. I made the decision. I bathed my body and cleaned my room so that no one would be left with the chore. I wrote letters to say goodbye, then tore them up and wrote them again. I hid them while I plotted a time my younger

106

siblings would be gone, and then I chose the least messy method of stopping my beating heart so that my mother would only see the peace of a sleeping body.

I wondered if I smiled towards the end, if my mouth would do me the great favor of maintaining it. In all of it, I did not want to hurt anyone, but how could I not see that the loss of me would be the greatest hurt? "Oh, Dustin, my baby brother... the loss of you is nearly unbearable." As the thought escapes with my exhaled breath, I have the most beautiful picture in my head.

There is a bird...a little bird.

Her color, as plain as that of a paper bag, catches my attention, more so than if she were colorful. I watch her float from shoulder to shoulder, her wings mimicking that of a beautiful ray made of water. There she rests now, on an older woman's gray blazer, so close to her ear that the soft of the woman's white hair brushes the little bird's wing. The tiny beak starts moving, and although this woman doesn't seem to realize the bird is there, a smile spreads, ever slightly, through her mouth, spreading all the way to the corners of her eyes.

"But, does she not know she is drowning?" I wonder. The bird must be singing the song of the Sirens, the song that calls brave men peacefully into treacherous cliffs to perish. I quietly release the hand holding mine and let the current move me through the church as I pull myself forward, one pew to the next, until I can nearly touch the bird.

She turns to look at me with beautifully familiar eyes. They are golden-yellow and cast the sun's light on my face. Her song starts again: "Just close your eyes and breathe...now imagine your soul. There are infinite rooms made up of a lifetime of memories. They are all a part of you; both joy and pain. Some rooms have lost all light; but the light wants to flow back in."

I exhale everything trapped in my chest—the air, the fear, and the sadness—and like a newborn saying goodbye to his mother's womb, I allow the church to fade away as I listen to the bird sing in my ear and I feel the universe wrap its infinite arms around me. With the pull of the water gone, I release my grip of the pew, resting, finally; but then the warmth of the bird's eyes disappears and I feel unbearably chilly. Alarmed, I open my eyes and instinctively look behind me, imagining this is how the sailor feels as he is hitting the cliff.

The corridor is long, paralleled walls with doors on either side.

The walls are white, the floors are white, the ceiling tiles are white, the hand holding mine is white, and I might cut my own flesh to add even a small amount of color if a sharp object were available. It is all too sterile. Organized.

I turn my head to look around me, and the church is still there. Feeling caged again, the beat of my chest turns wild. Then, retreating, my mind busies itself with the counting of steps as I turn away from the church and choose the corridor. Step, pause, step, pause, step...I look from the hand in mine, up the arm, and around the strong shoulder to find the face of my old man.

"Daddy?" He smiles down at me, but his eyes are sad.

"This isn't real," I say in the eerily lit-up area of the nearly lifeless hallway, but we keep walking, so I keep counting as I imagine an army of reinforcement at our flank. Eleven, twelve, thirteen…as I speak their names, they come to life as they stand up and join in the procession, filling the once-empty space. I imagine the numbers dressed in simple linen suits with crisp white shirts, but I can't decide if the shirts should be tucked in or left free of the constraints of a belt.

My dad reaches down and covers my hands with both of his and looks into my eyes. He has looked at me this way before. I was just a kid. I had taken a fall, and the nurses needed to move me to a cold table and pull my leg straight to get a clear x-ray of my hip. As I lay screaming in pain, my old man took my hands with the same reassuring smile and the same sad eyes. Just as I knew it had to be done then, I know this has to be done now. We take the last three steps… thirty-three, pause, thirty-four, pause, thirty-five.

They stand there boldly: a pair of steel doors, cold and unfeeling, guarding the unknown. "I will go in with you; everything will be okay," my dad reassures. An alarm blares one loud cry as I hear the clanking of metal levers going to work relentlessly to force the lock of the gates I dread. We seem to wait an eternity while they try to open to us, as if questioning a second time if we are certain of our journey. "No, Dad!" I refuse. "I don't want to do this!"

From somewhere in the building, my fear is answered by a piercing scream. It never stops. It climbs into my ears and moves through my veins as it inches its way into my heart, moving in closer and closer. There it digs and digs until there is a hollow hole for it to nest in. My body begins to shake so violently, the glass from the windows above my head shatters into a million pieces and cover every inch of me.

Then a sob spills over: "No, not my son… No, no, no, no! This is not real! Dustin, come back!" She grabs me to keep from falling, my warm arm beneath her hands, and I repent.

"It was my fault, Mom. I am sorry!" The grief continues to pour from her soul and with each tear she sheds, the great hole in my heart expands, inch by inch, until a large section has been completely severed off from the rest. I stumble to the wall's edge and slide down all sixty-one inches that God granted me and press my cheek to the floor, begging an escape.

"Don't make me do this, again…please, Little Bird."

"Do you remember?" Her melody calms me.

"Yes, Little Bird," I whisper. "I remember the shattering sound the heart of a grieving mother makes. I remember being covered by it."

She continues, "Child, are you sure that is what you heard?"

I search my memory and shake my head. "Yes."

"I want you to reach for it. Take it in your hands, and look at it," she encourages. I take the broken heart into my hands and try to piece it back together. It keeps falling apart, no matter how I place the pieces back together. I cradle it as you would a broken child and bring it against the skin on my face.

"It's my fault…it's my fault…I'm sorry!" I am shamed, as my tears began to blanket the broken heart. I bring my hands close to my own chest and encourage what is broken to beat in sync with the drum in my ribcage.

"Tell me, how could it be your fault? Did you pull the trigger?" the bird softly questioned.

"No, but he told me things, things I should have picked up on. If I had been paying attention, I could have stopped him," I argued. "So, isn't it the same?"

"Is it?" Again, she doubts. Time takes over the moment, and I close my eyes and listen to the quiet, hoping I will find the truth there. I feel a warm hand on my cheek and I open my eyes and find my mother waiting at the other end of that touch. She places her hand over my heart and says, "Will you release the guilt of not being able to stop what happened?" Uneasily, I shift.

"I want to, but Dustin left a trail for me to follow. He chose the wrong sister to save him."

She closes her eyes and speaks to the fractured thing dying in my hands. "You are not responsible for Dustin's choice; with that truth, only light will remain here."

I feel the beginning of an easiness I have not felt in years, like opening the windows in a stuffy room. Gently, she places her hands over mine and weeps a thousand tears. "Let it out, Heather," she coaxes. "Set it free. Grief is not meant to be swallowed and kept neatly hidden away."

One by one, they fall from my cheeks to our hands. The great fracture down the center of the heart slowly disappears, and light fills my fingers and spreads into the colorless hallway, painting the walls with a bright light. She smiles at me, the kind of smile one offers when a baby takes her first breath.

"There now. See, letting it out is okay. Look at your heart." She points to the upper left corner of my torso, and I look inside and see where a broken section has come back to the whole. The seam of a large tear is still thick, but light pours into it.

And my hands are empty. "You heard my grief and tucked yours away. The shattering sound came from your heart, darling, but now it can fly free, and your heart can mend." She soothes me as she kisses the top of my head.

"Now that some truth fills your soul, I need you to walk into another room with me before you continue with your dad. The path seems dark and you will face the memory of a great pain. Remember: a great light is already there, and when you turn the light on, your fear will leave."

Her eyes gaze across the hallway to a black door with an intricately carved sign over the frame. *Poiné* was carved out of the thick wood, and even though I do not recognize the dialect, it makes me shiver.

"Is this the only way?" I wonder, and I dread learning the answer. She finds my gaze and whispers words I tuck away like a covenant between two souls that existed in one body for nine months and fourteen days. She takes my hand as I turn the heavy knob and step into the night.

I have been swallowed by the dark. If I have eyes, they won't open; or…there is nothing. All I am certain of is my giant head, bobbing back and forth, unravelling from my neck as its weight challenges the tiny vertebrae holding the two together, stretched thin and ready to snap.

I try to pull the enormous mass back up, but it doesn't budge. I think about the rest of me, as it all seems missing, then I feel it—a flutter where my chest should be. Little wings beat back and forth in a space that feels caged, moving air around and around, frantically picking up speed and velocity to press free.

Then, "No! You're okay. Pause. Breathe. Just breathe. Inhale, now exhale, again." The bird calms just a bit.

Maybe I am being born; I am wrapped inside a tiny universe where the dark is a warm blanket, counting down the hours of completion before it squeezes life so tightly that the only escape is OUT. As if on cue, I feel a pressure grip me so tight that the air stops. It would be morbid to imagine I have been swallowed by a snake, my head the last to be consumed, dangling, eyes bulging out, the serpent's belly gorged to the point of resting.

So…this is not that. This is birth. This is life, not death. The grip loosens. "Breathe. Again." The first wave of heaving brushes me gently, its stroke just soft enough to reach into my torso. The second wave comes in violently. I fold in two as my skin catches fire and the bird starts stomping through my chest. I fall and land with my cumbersome skull first. There is an explosion that travels from one ear to the other, a piercing sound. I try to cover my ears with my hands, but I don't have any.

I don't have any hands.

I cannot open my eyes, but I feel them weeping over my cheeks. I open my mouth to scream and taste salt as flesh clamps down over my face, prying through the crease between my lips, and I gag again. If I have a mouth, I might have teeth, so I bite down as hard as I can. Just as I get a good grip, I feel searing pain over my cheek with a loud pop and my insides finally spill out. The laboring is finally over, and I imagine what I look like to my maker: handless, both my skull and mouth leaking onto the ground. And then I hear…

I hear oil, jumping from the heat of cast iron, only to fall into it again. I hear the sizzle of a pan. I have heard this sound a thousand times. I smell corn…maybe cornbread. The sound of wood pressing against the pan, four—no—five times.

The floor is settling under someone's feet, shifting back and forth now away from the stove. I recognize the sticky linoleum against my face. My eyelids agree to part, just a hair, as the blow comes hard against my spine, and I realize I have a back.

"You will clean it up next time. Do you hear me?" she hisses, stooping down to my level. My eyes refocus, and I take in her short blond hair, hitting just above her brows, and the deep lines between her eyes. They are brown. "Get these clothes off of her. She wreaks."

I lose her face. As she shuffles off, the cold seeps into my bones.

I have never believed in hell and always imagine the dark to be a quiet place for light to be born; and still, I have found myself wrong. Again.

Rough hands yank me off of the floor and carry me down a long, steep stairwell. The creaking of the wood under the heavy feet of my captor cries out as we descend further and further down. This and heavy breathing are all I hear as we pass from the land of the living and I am tossed into this waiting place broken, cold, and wet from my own vomit.

It seems an eternity, and then I hear movement amongst the shadows and I fear the waiting is over. There was the slightest hope that I had been left, forgotten in the quiet. Voices, harsh with a sound disguised as laughter, moves closer and

I want to run. My heart climbs, demanding my reaction as I command my legs to move; lifeless, they give no response to my pleas.

He grabs me by my ankles and drags me the length of a bed, bile leaving a soured trail behind me.

"Please, No!" I beg over and over.

His hair is as black as coal, swallowing the darkness. The smile on his face, like that of a Cheshire cat, is twisted, anticipating. His eyes are small and beady, feasting on what he has caught, savoring the terror. He mocks me, "No, no, no..." the falsetto tone piercing and unyielding.

He starts to unbuckle his belt, slowly, watching my every move, my heartbeat pounding like a freight train in my chest. He fumbles with the button on his pants and then reaches for me.

I begin to scream, gasping for breath between my panicked pleas, the sour fluid persistent in the objective of my drowning.

He puts a pillow, reeking from the odor that was left from someone's filthy head, over my face and screams for me to shut up. Time keeps ticking: *Fifty-three, fifty-four, fifty-five...*I have never been able to hold my breath a full minute. *Fifty-six.* As my body is ripped apart, I want to die; and yet I keep gasping. *Fifty-seven...fifty-eight. Fifty-nine.* Bile creeps up the back of my throat, and I hear a slight gurgle and fancy I am drowning.

Drowning... somewhere in a church that now seems far away, there is another mother crying. Drowning. I can feel her. I remember the parking lot and the deep regret of running away. I can't give up. I try to remember the words my mother whispered in my ear in the great hallway: "From the moment light was created, the darkness could not stop the filling of it. The darkness has no power over you. In the end, there is nothing but light. Call it by name, and it will be present."

I imagine the never-ending love that brought me back from the horrors of the night that altered my life forever. No matter how humiliated I was over what was done to my body, no matter how I feared being close to death, my family walked through the pain with me. They never gave up. "Little Bird!" I scream as I fill my lungs. Just as the short hand of the clock rises to the top, the sun fills a memory that was once buried in shame, and the melody of healing fills this room...*sixty*.

I am here. I am living. I am loving. I am worthy. I step back over the threshold of the door that means *pain* and see new words forming in the wood. I reach up to touch the letters... *Epoulosi*, and I walk away with a smile, for—yes—the truth and understanding of one's value is healing.

I wrap my arms around my dad's waist, whispering, "I see one more door. You will go in first?"

Just like that, the lock releases on the large doors at the end of the hallway and we walk through. Before I can take a breath, we are standing there. I am torn for only seconds, looking at the still body lying on the gurney, feeling the regret that will immediately come if I do not reach for him. I tell my arm to move, and I drive my hand forward with more force than I imagine the last touch should carry.

"No, no, no, no, this isn't right! I want one more chance to do it again."

I am saddened. But it is done. We are nervously watching the white sheet pinned across his chest, which hides the gaping hole a sister and father should not see. Then I realize he is slightly warm. I press my hand to his forehead more firmly, and I place my other hand on my own head. "Nearly the same," I say. My mind appeals to my heart even as the nurse shakes her head solemnly. Nonetheless, I defiantly hope for a miracle.

I look more closely, wondering if they have it all wrong; after all, I've heard stories of the seemingly dead coming back to life. Why not his story? Why not?

But the longer I look, the more anxious I become to look away. You see, they are not wrong; he is warm, but somehow... lacking something. He is lacking everything. This is what I will always remember; this instant it became real. This, for me, is the moment my brother died.

I notice his bluish colored lips, just slightly parted, and I glimpse a recently chipped tooth. Images of his beautiful face crashing against a sink creep into my thoughts, and I mourn for how hard he must have fallen.

Then I argue with myself: "No, not here. Don't think about this here." But how can I not? I close my eyes this time and place my hands on either side of his face, take a deep breath, and then imagine him smiling. It is his goofy smile, the one I love most. I do what most people do when they are smiled at, and I smile back. Then I scold myself for being comforted by my own delusion.

"Dustin, I don't know how to do this!" I reel, as he lies there... silently.

He can't argue back. "Argue back...please," I plead. I inhale until my lungs are full and burning; trapped is the life that moves through my body, held hostage in my chest. The second I exhale is the second I accept this grief and let it wash back out. And I can't. Because, as much as I know it is impossible, I want a miracle. Hope is powerful. Right?

My touch glides from his angled face, slowly to his forehead where my hand rests briefly just over his eyes, then moves up toward the crown of his head, never losing contact with his skin. In this moment I am only five years old, touching his infant body for the very first time, exploring a tiny nose, mouth, and ears. In these seconds, he is new. He is just beginning. As my hand slows to a rest at the very top of him, my eyes fly open. "Wait. Why has your hair gotten this long? Why did you let it go?" The baby from a breath ago is gone.

The last few years, he has taken great strides with a razor to keep any new growth off, battling the inevitable receding hairline handed down through our mother's side. Instead of finding his familiar smooth skin at the top of his head, I now sensed the soft of new hair against my fingertips. New hair on a dead man...doesn't in this moment make sense.

I love his hair at this length. I allow myself a hint of comfort to mask the confusion as this part of him brushes the smooth of my skin. Hair always feels the same, whether someone's body is living or dying, even your little brother's. Why do I have to know this?

I think about his lack of interest in the things that always mattered, the distant look in his gaze when we talked, the frown in his eyes that countered the smile on his face, the talks about "Parting Glasses," and the sharing of songs that gave power in one's choices—even if that choice was dying—and I try to fathom that I didn't notice it, this change in him.

I break under the weight of his quitting. He deserted me. He deserted me with this sadness and pain that won't leave. He deserted all of us.

Or...did I desert him? No. I did not make this choice for him. I forgive myself, again, and again, and as many times as it takes.... And then I realize.

I have not forgiven him.

I feel the air escape my lips, and I am forced to inhale again. And again...and...until my breath has returned to the living.

There will be no miracle. And I am here. Pain has not killed me. Loss has not killed me. Maybe this is why I can finally breathe again, having this small, yet substantial familiarity of him—where he was and where I don't want to be. Maybe that is why I can finally let my grief pour out of me.

And then.

For our last minute, for the last sixty seconds with him, I want to close my eyes with my hand on his head and, for a second, pretend he is here.

And so I do.

I start counting again. In ten months, when he turns thirty-seven, he sits around the campfire with our family telling a story of a great heartbreak and his will to survive it. Thirty-eight: he pulls his daughter into his arms for the first time in years, and when she hugs him back, he is made whole. Forty: I look into his eyes and marvel at his baby face and dimpled cheeks, never aging as the peace in his heart grows vast.

Fifty: I stand on the ground with his sons and watch above as his slim body flies over Christ the Redeemer like a magical human bird. Sixty-three: he climbs the most glorious peak at sunset, the digging of his walking stick leaving marks in the earth.

Seventy-eight.

Eighty-Seven.

And finally... Ninety. He sits at the side of my bed and caresses my dying hand as he bids me farewell looking into my tired, yet full eyes. He sits at the side of my bed, because baby brothers are not supposed to die first.

"Has it been a lifetime yet?" I demand from beyond that touch to whoever is in charge. "Does he continue to circle the sun at a pace that takes a dozen months? Does he walk his daughter down the aisle and watch his sons turn into men? Does he conquer his fears and find peace in his heart? Does he? Does his skin age soft with wrinkles as he holds his grandchildren and remembers the miracle of life? Tell me, please...does he?"

No. He does not. And this is the end. This is the last minute.

My dad's hand on my shoulder startles me back to this chilly room that I will never unfeel, no matter how many lifetimes I live, no matter how many smiles cross my face. I look all around me and allow myself the frivolous comfort of imagining he could still be here. I breathe my words out into the atmosphere, hoping they will find their way to him.

"I love you, little brother."

Then, again, I hear the bird singing from far away. As in a dream, I watch the hospital room fade around me and I am in utter darkness. The little bird has taught me how to turn the light on, so I know the darkness is grasping at these last few moments, and I am not scared.

I pray, "Little brother...I am sorry I was not light in the right moment. Please forgive me. But keep hope. I will be for someone, for as many people that will let me put my arms around them. I forgive time for taking you. I forgive our creator for not healing you, and I forgive you for quitting. I am shutting all of these doors and walking into light. Until we meet again, little Monkey. Love, your big Sis."

I feel a nudge at my hand, and with this simple touch, a small light turns on in the deepest part of my heart. There in the shadows is the same warm smile she had given me earlier in the sanctuary just after we were seated for the memorial. My heart begins to warm like a crackling fire until I can see everything around me again. The little bird is seated on her shoulder, tucked in close to her neck, and when she looks me in the eye, the bird follows suit. When she opens her mouth to say, "I love you," the little bird sings the melody that means *I love you*. Then she takes my arm and leads me out of this place that should bring peace but many times brings pain.

As I remember the little bird, I think, "That, would be the greatest superpower of all, to be a voice in the dark. I want to be like that which moves with wings and sings with the rhythm of peace. I want to be the voice of hope."

When I sat in the dark of my nightmares and the cold of the surgical room, I saw hope as one thing: the wanted miracle. My perspective of hope was having faith in the outcome I longed for. I realize that hope is much more than what we muster when we lose control. It is more than wishes and wants and prayers tossed out into space. Hope is not most

121

powerful in the miracle. Hope is most powerful when you have faith that you will survive when there is no miracle.

I wish my heart could sense hopelessness in every soul. I wish I could fly close to each ear and sing a song that will bring light into seemingly lifeless eyes that are imprisoned in dark places. I wish I could defeat the lie that says, "You are not worthy," and sing the melody that reminds us that it is in the dark that light shines the brightest and, in the light, we can see our worth.

For me, happiness exists in the light of forgiveness, hope, and love. If we love, we have all things. Love is the greatest treasure of life.

"If you want something,
go get it period."

~ Chris Gardner

CHAPTER EIGHT

THE TASTE OF DIRT

By Sadie Konrad

I fell. For about the thirteenth time that day, I fell. I didn't see the gash on my knee, and I couldn't hear the onlookers asking if I was okay. All I could see was that accursed finish line, an ideal example for the phrase "so close and yet so far," as it sat at the bottom of the hill with about a mile of twisting red-dirt switchbacks to get there.

This was the spring of my senior year of high school, and I was a cross-country mountain bike racer. I was on a team with about forty other riders from my school, and we competed against racers from all across the state. It was the first race of my final season with the league, and I was coming in dead last. Now, I'm not talking photo-finish last. I'm talking last as in so-far-behind-that-people-thought-you-died last, or as in the-vendors-are-packing-and-leaving last.

Our local Southern California sun was coming down in full swing, with the brush and twigs along the paths being the kind of dry that causes the whole environment to latch onto your shorts and socks, and the heat being so that your skin becomes burnt just by sitting near a window. I was shaking and crying, covered so thickly in a tan dust that you could hardly see the red of my racing jersey, as I fumbled helplessly with my bike chain. It had fallen off its track and had become lodged between the gears. I frantically tried to rip it loose, knowing that the god-forsaken finish line was just a few hundred feet away now. Spectators on the side tried desperately to give me instructions in an attempt to save me from a nearing emotional shutdown as my grease-covered gloves tugged and pried at the gears to no avail.

It hadn't always been this way, I assure you. Not to say that it was never hard because it always was. But the added misery and shame was a new feature of race day. In years past, I was a strong athlete, sometimes even vying for one of the top placements, with the leader's podium always a little closer to grasp. I was happy being out there among the dirt and the rocks, and I was even happy to come home with a few scrapes every now and again. I was happy doing something where I felt so in control, yet so *not* in control, where everything could change in an instant. It was the thrill of the unknown, that's what I was racing for. The chance of falling short or the possibility of surpassing everyone's expectations and absolutely soaring. Granted, I was never a star by any means. Still, though, I was at one point so, so close to the top.

But I fell.

And when you fall from that high up, you land in a crumpled ball of a person in the dirt, looking up at the sky at all you could have had.

It was only two years before this that I had first gotten into mountain biking, and truthfully it was completely by accident. I was fifteen and had just gotten dumped by my very first boyfriend, and being the preteen that I was, of course I thought my life was over. Most of my friends were his friends, most of my activities were his, and we had classes together. I knew I wanted to take a leap into something different, to discover what happiness truly meant when it came from within me rather than it being reliant on anything else.

I thought of a few other sports or teams around school, but I never had the courage to inquire about any of them. I figured that all of the girls had already been doing that sport or activity since they were seven; meanwhile, the last time I even touched a soccer ball was when I was six.

I remember going home and taking out my beach cruiser to ride around town, which was probably the thing I enjoyed doing most. I would have a little portable radio in the basket and listen to music while I rode around. I learned all the bike paths, the street names, and if I didn't know what a building was, I would go inside and ask. I had been doing this for a while, because every birthday, I would ask for my riding radius to be stretched out just a little farther, and I would explore that part of town, always on my own and always with music.

What I know now is that this was my first experience with real adventure. I took myself where I wanted to go, and I even had the power to decide how fast I wanted to get there. In fact, I would say this one of my first tangible experiences with "the thrill of the chase," so to speak. At this stage, being so young, I think all I really knew was that I was happy and didn't really look into it any deeper than that. At fifteen, I'm pretty sure that's how we all are. I had a pretty raw idea of what happiness was to me, but it still required some fine tuning to figure out what it was about biking that I truly enjoyed the most.

When I saw a poster in the school hallway for a cross-country mountain bike team in need of female riders, all I knew was I needed some new friends and riding my bike made me happy. I had no idea just how much my definition of happiness itself would change along the way.

After school, I went to the classroom listed, walked through the open door, and saw an older man sitting at a desk in the corner of the room, head down and looking at a stack of papers. His peppered grey hair showed the life he had led, and he wore a short-sleeved button-down, revealing arms that reflected all his days in the sun.

"Do you run the mountain bike team?" I asked.

He raised his head from his papers. "Yes, that's me. I'm Mr. Lewis. Were you interested in joining the team? It's more of a club anyways. The school won't let us call it an official team."

I smiled, but not wishing to waste any of his time or further my embarrassment, I cut straight to it. "Do you need any experience to join the team?"

He sat up a bit straighter before very slowly and firmly stating, "You do not need any experience at all."

This was the start of an all-new chapter in my life, one covered in big laughs, road trips to middle-of-nowhere competitions, and singing along to songs I hadn't heard before—all with people I wondered how I had gone my entire life without. On a team of 40 riders, I was one of only six girls, three of whom were also brand-new to the team. I was expecting to only feel comfortable around the new girls, figuring the boys would likely keep to themselves, especially since I didn't know anything about riding or mechanics or anything else a racer might need to know. But no matter what situation I found myself in, whether it was trying to put my bike on a car rack for the first time or my initiating, scar-producing crash, there was never a shortage of good people helping me.

Not only that, I watched my whole way of life transform. That happiness that came from riding my bike around became more precise. Sure, it was great that I was getting exercise, but that wasn't what it was. And of course, the music aided the aesthetic, but that wasn't it either. It was that feeling of intense freedom and discovering the natural beauty that was all around. It was a period of time I look back on now in shades of pastel purple sunsets covering the sandy hills and scraggly bushes in a dusk worthy of a painting every evening. It was early morning rides where your lungs haven't quite woken up yet, and it hurts just to ride and breathe at the same time.

It was the outdoors and the desperate need to get amongst it.

The first season came and went, as did the following, and my skills on a bike grew parallel to my relationship with my team, riders and coaches alike. I remember how excited they would always be throughout races, running alongside me and cheering me on, holding up whiteboards and hands to let me know what place I was in. They even had radios they used to talk to each other and update everyone on how we were doing. They would scream and clap and beam and make us feel like we were made of magic.

At the end of my second season, approaching my third and final one, tensions were a bit higher. I had to accumulate a certain number of points and hold a high enough placement if I wanted to qualify to race in the varsity division. And if I did, I would be the first woman in my high school's history to do so. I remember after my last race, coming in 11th place and re-checking my math over and over and over again, calculating my overall placement... and not believing that I had made it.

I had done it. It was the end of the season, and I was happy. I was thrilled, of course, to be doing so well, but I had found this thing that I loved, with new people that I loved and new places that I loved. And because of that, I was simply, immeasurably happy.

But I fell.

Now, there is, without a doubt, a certain amount of fear we all carry when we set out to try new things. For some, this feeling is often accompanied by exhilaration, but for others, it's a form of paralysis. The thing of it is, though, when we try new things, we often forget that no one expects perfection from us. Whether it's a new sport, learning a new language, or having someone teach you to drive a manual, there is generally someone there to graciously teach you the ropes.

That being said, I think there is a deeper fear that we have the ability to feel—not the fear that comes with being new and making mistakes—but fear of making mistakes knowing full-well that we ought to know better. Haven't you noticed how this idea can hold you back from happiness in your own life? Often, we find ourselves sitting in our own misery, something invisible to those around us because it is completely fabricated. Even if you know what makes you happy, there is this invisible thing holding you back.

I think there are many people who allow the taunts from

inside their own heads to choke out their inner happiness. It is a slithering type of fear that lies and tells us to hide away in shame, away from those we love and away from the joy we feel we don't deserve. I often wonder how many memories, moments, and people I have missed out on while living with this notion.

And so it was my first race of my final season, and I fell.

See, the summer before that last season, I decided to take on a job so I could be prepared to pay my way through college. I worked at a local fast food chain, where you got a free double cheeseburger and fries every shift that you worked. And since I often worked after practice (or in place of practice), I'm sure you can see where this story goes.

I ended up practically clawing through the finish line on hands and knees with about a thousand things I needed to address, from the rip in my jersey to the water I so desperately needed. I still wanted to be with my team and support them, but I dared not tell a soul how my own race had gone. And I sure as hell did not want to make eye contact with my coaches.

I knew I had to get better before the next competition, but the following race was only two weeks away, which, of course, was upon us all in the blink of an eye. I was riding every day that I had off, and even on some of the days I didn't. I was getting up before class to work out at the school gym and riding during the time I had between school and work. I traded French fries for celery sticks, milkshakes for green smoothies... the whole bit.

I knew it really couldn't make an enormous difference in just two weeks, but I thought that if perhaps I kept good habits up, then I wouldn't feel as down about my placement, knowing I had truly tried my best to change for the better. Even at this point in time, I was trying to convince my mind that I deserved to be happy, no matter my placement. I was caught up in this idea of earning grace, working towards acceptance from others when I hadn't even accepted myself, let alone any kind of self-forgiveness. Although I had already set my bad habits in the past, I was still living in that mindset, focusing on the negative and not furthering my own pursuit of happiness. Pursuing, by definition, requires that one must go forward, does it not?

Then, it was time for all of that to be put to the test. Even today, the thought of hearing the announcer counting down the racers is enough to get my heart pounding. You stand with your bikes in rows of four, with one foot on the pedal and one foot on the ground, trying to steady your breathing as the announcer describes the course.

"Racers will go up Ambulance Trail, pass the Tunnel of Love section, and continue onto the Tarantula downhill, which will connect with Tunnel of Love. Be sure to watch for riders on your right when you enter."

You check your gearing for the thousandth time, praying that it's just right for this kind of start.

"Varsity Girls, you are doing three laps. Each lap is about 5.5 miles. If you need a refill on water, be sure to stay towards the right side of the track past the finish line."

You could hear a pin drop. You look around at the girls in front of you, to your left, to your right, and behind. It's going to be a mess, having twenty riders lined up like soldiers about to go ballistic on the signal.

"Alright, here we go. Five, four, three, two, one…"

And they're off.

The thing of it is that when I started this sport, I began with nothing. I didn't have the right kind of bike, gloves, helmet, clothes, shoes, or bike rack. And I certainly didn't have any knowledge or skills to speak of. I had nothing to offer but my willingness to work and an optimistic attitude. Coach Brett lent me his wife's bike for my whole first year of riding. Coach Dennis gave me a pair of riding glasses. Coach Mason helped me with my pedals more times than I can count, and Coach Mark was the one who helped connect me to a sponsor who was willing to pay for half of a brand-new bike, one made just for me and my shorter-than-average stature. And it was my favorite color.

They had given me, quite literally, my world. I could have never gotten into the sport on my own, if not for the lack of equipment, then for the lack of experience. The only friends I had at the time were on the team, and they were some of the truest people I have ever met.

People were always commenting how lucky I was to find something so great at such a young age, as well as a sport I could stick with even after high school or even beyond college. Some of those closer to me noticed how much healthier my body looked, but there was not a soul around who didn't notice the change in my spirit, with eyes constantly looking towards the horizon, wondering what could possibly be out there. And it might not have ever happened, because I really didn't deserve any of it.

But Coach Brett spent hours training me how to nail sharp turns with some cones in a parking lot. Mason told me that if I could talk to my friends on the uphill, I wasn't pedaling hard enough. Dennis took all the newer riders on the same trail over and over when we were learning how to downhill, refusing to let us leave without a boost in confidence. And on race day, Coach Mark, in a firetruck-red jersey, would make sure we had everything we needed, from a clean bike chain, properly filled tires, even new handlebar grips if he thought it would make a difference. His face would light up when I turned the corner he was standing on. "You're my hero!" he would always say, fists in the air, while my teammates ran alongside the track clapping and screaming like the teenagers they were.

That's why, in this moment, I owed it to them to try to give them back even half an ounce of what they had given me.

But it was so hot.

We were off and, as if on cue, my head started to play tricks on me—from constantly feeling like my chain had popped off when it hadn't to constantly feeling like I needed water when the race had only just begun. Despite these irrational and incredibly invasive mental blocks, I noticed I was doing okay. Sure, I was still in last place, but I felt strong. On some of the straighter sections, I could even see the girl in front of me.

Nonetheless, I didn't expect my teammates or anyone other than my family to be watching me anymore, as my races had become quite uneventful. I didn't expect to hear my name announced and discussed by the scorekeepers. I didn't expect my coaches to cheer. After all, I wasn't made of magic anymore.

I had just passed the finish line and was beginning lap two. I kept on pedaling hard, in a gear so low that sometimes I had to stand up just to get enough weight to drive the pedals down. But I was beyond the point of accepting anything less now. I didn't deserve any recognition for it, but I would be damned if I wasn't going to leave every ounce of my being on the dirt that day. After all, she was right there in front of me.

She in her yellow jersey, ponytail hanging out of her matte black helmet.

I went through a dip, clenching my handlebars in my fists with white knuckles, as though that would somehow make me faster.

She turned a corner, disappearing behind a mound of rocks and weeds. I pedaled hard to get around the bend and see my opponent again, but as I made the turn and began the descend, my bike caught a rock.

And I fell.

My front tire had stopped in the ground, my body flinging over the handlebars and hitting the ground with a quick, loud smack.

It's hard to recall precisely what happened next, although I'm fairly certain I screamed. I was bitter, dismal, heartbroken, and angry. I wasn't afraid or hurt in an incapacitating way, but I did spend a moment there deciding what to do, as there were two basic options I knew of: I could get back on the bike and finish, or I could get back on the bike and race.

A third option I thought about for a solid few minutes, was getting back on the bike, riding straight to the car and deleting my coaches' numbers from contacts. Asking the question now, as I sit here writing this, the answer seems obvious. But standing there exhausted, covered in dirt and rocks and blood, knowing that one way or another I had to get to the finish line, I wanted just to cut my losses and start walking my bike down the hill.

I stood up and looked myself over, picked up my bike, and after seeing no deal-breaking injury to person or cycle, I got back on and started pedaling, still unsure of how I wanted to proceed.

At the bottom of the hill, I started to see civilization again. I heard the sound of people shaking cowbells and shouting, even the announcer off in the distance. I passed a course marshal, a couple of spectators from various teams, and then I finally saw a familiar face in a bright red jersey.

Coach Mark was there on the sidelines talking with a few spectators, not really paying much attention. I tried to steady my breathing, wondering if it was at all possible to ride by him without him noticing me covered in dirt and sprinkled with blood, huffing and puffing in last place. But, as it would seem, bright red jerseys are hard to miss.

He turned his head and saw me and began cheering along with the others around and clapping slowly. "Great job, Sadie. Way to go!" he said.

I was happy for the acknowledgment but still embarrassed and ashamed, so I kept my head down and pedaled on.

Then, I wasn't sure if it was something I did, or perhaps something I didn't, but all of a sudden, his applause became louder. It was only then that I realized he was running alongside me, still cheering me on. I looked up at his face and saw that same, big old smile he'd shown me when I had placed among the leaders, and he was running and yelling as though he genuinely was thrilled at my performance.

"You're my hero!" he yelled in between some laughs and "wahoos."

And just like the sort of magic that was apparently abundant on competition days, I was racing.

My happiness didn't come from Coach Mark's approval. It didn't come from a good placement or even the acknowledgement of my teammates. It was that thrill of the chase that came with all.

Still though, imagine trying to watch your favorite movie, except that they switched out all the actors and removed the soundtrack. Sometimes, we can know exactly where our happiness lies, but we allow all sorts of things to get in our way of that search. Oftentimes, we allow ourselves to live in a state of mind that we feel we deserve. This place, often abrasive and destitute, is where we keep ourselves from being happy or from even pursuing the idea of happiness, becoming so lost in our shame that we feel it is our sealed destiny to be miserable.

I could not believe that Coach Mark would actually be happy with me after all that I had done, but this was never his fault. I got in my own way. If I had simply faced my fears and spent time with my coaches and my team, despite my past mistakes and current flaws...I wonder how many laughs and hugs I have robbed myself of by living in such a hopeless state of mind?

I'm not sure if he ever knew or if I ever even told him, but that moment changed everything for me. I snapped out of my daze in that instant and found new motivation and power to compete, not only that day but in the final races following it. It wasn't some miraculous change you might see in Hollywood where the lead character goes from zero to hero, but I did improve my placements by coming in fourth from last instead of dead last, and I felt more confident and ready on the courses, both mentally and physically.

I ended that season happily. I had a love and appreciation for my team, the coaches, the sport, and everything you ought to be happy about your senior year. Looking back, I am often reminded of something my pastor said in a message once: "God cleans His fish after He gets them in the boat."

Many people often feel that they can't come to God or even think about the idea of Him because of all the mistakes they've made and where they have been. Many decide to take it upon themselves to straighten out their lives before making a decision to follow Jesus. The problem with that thinking is, the moments where we have everything in our lives perfectly set are rare and far between.

This analogy proved true even in my small little team. I knew that I had slipped up, but rather than simply going to my team and coaches for help, I tried to fix the problem privately, in self-imposed exile, which only made the problem worse, with the added hurt of damaging my relationship with the friends around me who just wanted to help. Not to mention that the entire prospect of seeking a grace I couldn't even earn was an enormous detour from seeking out happiness for myself in the first place.

And so, when competing was finally done and behind me, I kept riding, finally enjoying my sport for what it was again. My bike took me into emerald green forests, alongside dry, sandy hills, and to the ridges overlooking my hometown to watch the sunrise. One other place my bike took me that following year, if you could believe it, was back at the races, wearing a bright colored coaching jersey that hung just a tad too loose on my short and slightly boyish stature.

I was attending a community college not too far away from my old world of bikes and dirt, so I had the opportunity to come back as a coach in the league alongside a team of coaches, some familiar to me and some new. Since I still wasn't fast enough to train the faster kids on my new little team, I was usually assigned to work with the newer, more timid riders, and I would not give those months away for the world. I knew from my experiences what it was like to start fresh, a forgiven person trying his absolute best to improve every day.

But what really drove this lesson home was being given the opportunity to watch it come full circle as I found myself helping these young kids, scared out of their minds, and being able to show them that it is okay to make mistakes no matter who you are, teaching them to be happy no matter what state they found themselves in. I so desperately wanted each of them to know that they were just as much of a racer as the others, that we wanted to see them at practice no matter where they were emotionally, and that I was always proud of them no matter how they did. I tried to make them feel magical, and looking back today, I hope with all of my might that they understood.

I've heard it said that the most reassuring phrases in the world are the words "me too" and "me neither." Whether you are confiding in a classmate that you haven't started the project yet or wondering if someone has made the same mistakes as you, it is always comforting to know we are not alone in our endeavors. We all mess up, and it's okay to be embarrassed about some of our blunders. The problem only occurs when we allow this embarrassment to grow larger than we are, becoming impossible for one person to overcome. And shame is a cruel thing to sentence anyone to, especially for life, especially alone, and especially if it's yourself.

Find your courage, show humility, ask forgiveness, and move on. And when it's your turn and someone is coming to you this way, show mercy and grace and love. When they mess up and have to come to you again, forgive them twice. It's a very difficult thing to try and fly while clinging to the weights you swear have enslaved you.

But you know something? Life just isn't that long. There is a whole treasure trove of new experiences and new happiness waiting for you, if only you would drop the weights. The sooner you can let go, the sooner your hands will be free to reach out and grab something beautiful. And if it is not beautiful, let it go and try again.

Gather ye rosebuds while you may

Old Time is still a-flying;

And this same flower that smiles today

Tomorrow will be dying.

("To the Virgins, To Make Much of Time" –Robert Herrick)

"Put your happiness in no one else's hand but your own."

~ Unknown

CHAPTER NINE

My Journey to Happiness

By Annette Forsythe

Once upon a time, there was a young woman who fell in love with the man of her dreams. They got married, lived in a beautiful house, had the perfect children, and lived happily ever after. ~ The End.

If it were only that simple. Life has a way of playing its hand and there are many bumps and bruises that get in the way of that perfection. It's not a bad thing, just real. We don't come with rose-colored glasses.

Miriam Webster defines happiness as the state of being happy, contentment, pleasure, satisfaction, joyous, light-hearted well-being. Aristotle defined happiness not as a state but an activity.

There are clichés stating that it can't be bought by money, that it's a choice, or it can be found in lemonade. A child's mind can find happiness in the simplest pleasures. Even Charles Schultz has a song about happiness in his play *You're a Good Man Charlie Brown*. But it doesn't seem that easy or clear-cut as we get older; there are so many more factors to consider. Me, I believe happiness comes from within. We make our own happiness from the way we approach our lives.

Happiness is a feeling that comes from the deepest part of your soul, that guides the way you live, act, and feel. It's about being at peace and finding the joy that's all around you, living in a state of gratitude with a heart that is full of love and contentment.

I have read a number of articles and blogs in *Psychology Today* on this very subject. Even though every person has his or her own way to define happiness, I could not help but notice the common threads that include both emotion and feelings. Scientists, economists, psychologists, and even Buddhist monks have summed it up as something that is deep and deliberate: that happiness encompasses living a full, meaningful life using one's gifts and time to live with thought and purpose.

I think it can get tricky when emotion and your state of mind intermix. There have been times when I was happy but did not have happiness, moments when I have laughed on the outside but have been heartbroken inside. Put a smile on your face or a hop in your step. You must be happy! How easy it is to play on this term, this feeling that depends on circumstance and frame of mind.

I had to dig into this train of thought a little more. Back to the dictionary: emotions are feelings; a state of mind is a function. Feelings are temporary and shape our outlook, and a state of mind lasts longer and is more pervasive. Feelings can transition to your state of mind, and your state of mind influences how you interact with others. Got all that? My logical mind can follow, but my emotional Italian mind does not.

I have asked myself if I am happy, but what is happiness? There is not a sign that flashes "happiness here." There are

144

money and possessions and actions, moods and moments, etc., but these are things and we have feelings about them. None of this resonates deep in my soul. What does happiness look like?

Is it possible to look at someone and see that they are happy? I am sure there are scientific observations that show how happiness can affect the brain, how it looks a certain way at a molecular level in a microscope. But on a purely unscientific level, what are the outward signs? I really don't believe there is a happiness gesture, but the way we live and present ourselves could suggest we live in a state of happiness. Smiles can come and go, tears of joy wiped away, we don't have happiness uniforms. What is this subjective frame of mind, how do we achieve it, and—more importantly—how do we maintain it?

Still questioning where my happiness comes from, my next step was to look at all the phases of my life. I am told I was a happy baby. But an infant's needs are simple. Their smiles come as freely as their love. A clean diaper and a full belly bring them contentment.

I was a happy child. I knew I was loved, had lots of friends, played outside, did things with my family. I had everything I needed. I was happy. It was simple. Even in the midst of teenage angst there was happiness. I learned to drive, had more freedom, earned my own money, belonged to clubs, and had a select few good friends. And I still knew I was loved at home. How could it get any better?

As a young adult, there was college, parties, music, clubbing, a car, boys, experimenting with my newfound freedoms. Yup, it's still all good, and through it all I was still strengthened by the love of family. Even as a young married, I was blinded by love. The anticipation of the future—having children, buying a home, living in my perfectly euphoric state—of course I was happy! I knew I would live in my dream world forever.

But then once I got here and reached this stage of my life, something happened. It wasn't so simple anymore. I had so many romantic ideals about how every part of my life would play out. The novelty of perfection started to fade. I started living in the real world, where life gets in the way and things are not the way you'd always dreamed they would stay. Oh, I had plenty of happy times, but that did not create happiness. There were way too many emotions involved.

I married my college sweetheart. He is my best friend. Life was perfect; my dreams had come true, just like in the magazines or on the Hallmark Channel. But reality had a different agenda for us. There were to be a few challenges ahead.

We started a family right away. My children are my joy! I cannot begin to describe the wonder and gift of being a mom—the wonder that comes with watching their journeys. My husband is a devoted dad, involved, a wonderful life mate, and a completely functional alcoholic. My perfect world had a demon named vodka, and this became the dirty little secret I dedicated myself to hiding. There were plenty of happy times, but all the while I lived in fear of the secret coming out. We were this picture-perfect family. I couldn't let what went on behind closed doors be exposed.

This went on for years, living in underlying fear of what would cause the next outburst. I thought I had done a good job of protecting my girls only to find out they knew everything and carried their own scars. My own family avoided being around because they couldn't bear to see me hurt. I felt completely alone. This was when I needed their unconditional love the most.

Before I continue, make no mistake, I was not a wallflower during this time. There were as many happy memories made as bad ones. We were in love and shared a strong partnership. He could make me laugh like no other. I was involved in plenty of things, had lots of friends, and actively volunteered in my community. I was busy raising my family and being involved in their lives. Actually, so was my husband. He coached, was on the Board of Education, and was the other half of my divide-and-conquer act. The only problem was, we were never sure if he would be sober or not. If you weren't privy to the tells, you would think everything was fine.

There are plenty of stories that I could share about the drunken antics, but it really would not add any value. I still loved him and wanted to protect him in the midst of all my hurt and anger. Such is life with a codependent and an alcoholic. We were quite the pair.

When his health became an issue and he was told to get sober or die, things eventually changed. Even that journey followed a crooked path, but sobriety followed for ten beautiful years. They were happy years where I found the man I married, my best friend, the one who put the stars in my eyes.

I learned a lot about myself in that time. I realized I could never go back to that other life again. It was very easy to set that boundary when it wasn't challenged and to feel confident about it. This time the fear was for the dreaded relapse, if it should ever come. That fear just got put away in its own little compartment and forgotten.

I think it would be fair to say I may have slipped back in to my perfect world during this time. It was like I was that 23-year-old bride all over again. But—wait for it—that would not last long enough. Life came back with a vengeance. My youngest brother-in-law passed on the same day we found out our youngest daughter had thyroid cancer. Just weeks later, our first grandchild was stillborn, and there, my friends, was the one-two-three punch to the gut. It did not take long for the downhill spiral to start from there.

My husband immediately began to self-medicate. I kept feeling the sense of his drinking, but, after all these years, how could that be possible? This went on for over a year. I couldn't possibly hurt him by asking if he was drinking; that would be cruel. What kind of a suspicious witch was I? I refused to suspect he could break his promises to me. Denial at its finest! Until I started finding the empties.

My father had come to visit. He was 90 and in ill health. Old fashioned, stubborn, and a little demanding, to say the least. Sadly, he spent most of that summer in the hospital with pneumonia. When I wasn't at work, I was at his bedside. With my not being around, my husband did not have to even try to hide that he had relapsed. By the time I got home at night, he was deep asleep.

But when Dad was finally well enough to come home, not hiding had become the new habit.

The behavior was blatant, verbally abusive, and mean. My husband did not care who saw or heard what he had to say. My dad was heartbroken to hear anyone talk to or treat me in that manner.

I remember the night I finally had the courage to ask the question that had haunted me for 35 years. Knowing I could not live like this again, I told him he could not have it all. Was it me or the bottle? My worst nightmare came true that night when he chose the bottle. Things just continued to deteriorate as I tried to figure out my next steps. We hadn't even hit rock bottom yet.

Dad's health continued to fail, my husband and I were living separate lives under the same roof, and I was desperately trying to find the courage to leave. I drove around with half of my belongings in my trunk for longer than I care to admit. I felt completely pathetic at this time, like a laughing stock. Who sticks around to be treated in this manner? Was I that desperate? I took vows, for better or worse. God was certainly showing me the worst, but those vows were as sacred to me then as they are now. I was fighting for our life, our memories, everything we had built together.

When my dad passed, I was away from home. I called to tell my husband. I knew he was drunk. He said all the things he was supposed to say. But the next morning, not only had he not told our daughter, he had forgotten that Dad had passed. Now we hit rock bottom. I could have cared less if he even came to the funeral. But he did come, and as much as I hate to admit it, I needed him and his support. I wouldn't have gotten through it without him. That is when he started realizing he did not want to be that person. It still wasn't a straight path to his sobriety, but it was a start.

He "didn't need help." He "had done it before." He "had it under control." Or not. This hero mentality went on for months. I had reached a breaking point. But love and brutal honesty kept me present. I had been in counseling for over a year at this point, and then I found this personal development program. The overlap was incredible. Step by step, I started putting myself together again, finding my voice, my spunk, and my determination. There would be no looking back from now on.

The lesson learned, even though there were hard circumstances, realizing that every time I pointed my finger, there were three more pointing back at me. You mean to tell me that I shared responsibility for my lack of happiness? Mind boggling! But true. If I was going to make a decision to stay, then I had to find a way to meet him in the middle somehow.

I did a lot of soul-searching. I had to come to accept that alcoholism is an illness, and just as hard to kick as staying on a diet. I blamed my husband for everything that went wrong during this tumultuous period in our marriage. But damn if I didn't have to own it also! That is not an easy admission, my friends. After all, I was playing the most graceful victim. But that had to stop. It was time to take responsibility. Reconciliation would be the only acceptable outcome.

Mind, body, and soul. Where do you start? What needs the most help? I found a nutritional program that nourished my body, which by this time was literally falling apart. My stress levels were through the roof. I had gained a ridiculous amount of weight. My blood pressure was high. I went into heart failure, developed blood clots and several autoimmune disorders, and began downing a handful of medications that rivaled my dad's. Hold on! How could this be my life?

So, as a tool in this nutritional plan, there was a program that was to help reset your mindset and change how you approach the ways you live and take care of your health. I dove in, and that was the beginning of taking back control of my life. After completing this program, I was directed to a group called Growth-U. Some may call it personal development, or life lessons, or hocus-pocus. It doesn't matter, because these programs have been the greatest gifts I have ever given myself.

I am worth the time and effort it takes to make myself the best I can be. I have developed tools to be strong. I have learned to move forward and put the past where it belongs. I live every day with a heart full of love, and if someone hurts me, I recognize it as their cry for help and pour all my love in to them. I have learned forgiveness from a whole new level. Forgiving myself as well as others. I have accepted our humanness and that we all just do the best we can do. I spend my days looking for ways to add value in every manner I can think of. Pay it forward. Hold on to those words, because everything you give comes back to you tenfold. This is how I found my truest meaning to happiness: from the inside out, making it about others.

I will proudly tell you that my husband is going to five meetings a week. My heart bursts every time he is a guest speaker, sharing his story and his recovery. I am so proud of his efforts to take a healthy lifestyle seriously. After 38 years of marriage, we are probably closer than we have ever been. I know we are certainly more honest with each other than ever. And we both continue to grow everyday. Our tools may be different, but the end product is the same. We are both working toward our best life. His friend is Bill, and my friend and mentor is Rod Hairston. Even though our journeys are different, we are taking them hand in hand.

I had to accept our humanness, that we were both doing our best and it wasn't necessarily going to be an easy journey, but we would be together supporting one another all the way. Living in a state of perfect imperfection is a crazy kind of blessing, and I am so grateful I get to share it with my best friend. There will be slips, and there will be denial, but there will also be the space to love and forgive. Self-love and forgiveness are pretty steep hurdles to get over. You can't be happy if you don't take care of yourself and honor that you are human. You must believe in all the possibilities. The future is yours to envision. You get to write your own story.

Mine is not to be interpreted as a sad story. This is my journey, all the good, bad, and ugly of it. How I found my way to a life that is not only happy but filled with happiness. Now, if I were to ask myself if I had happiness, I know my answer is an emphatic YES! I have purpose, contentment, and joy that comes from the very root of my being. Who would have ever thought my happiness would come from my perfectly imperfect reality?

I have never known this kind of peace and fulfillment before. I don't even know the words to describe the contentment in my soul. As a person who could "talk to the nails on the wall," being speechless is a big statement. I want everyone to know the happiness I carry because is it equally attainable for all.

I start every day with self-love. I meditate each morning before I get up. I count my blessings and give thanks every day for my husband, my life, and my family. I choose to be happy. It is the small changes to my mindset that keep me focused on positive emotions. The Serenity Prayer is a constant reminder of the fragile balance and it strengthens me every time my old patterns start to show up.

Even in the midst of your greatest sorrows, signs appear. Keep faith. Finding your true happiness is not an enigma. You just have to be open to the possibilities and forge ahead.

Footnote:

Webster's Third New International Dictionary, Unabridged; April 2016; unabridged.merriam-webster.com

Carlin Flora; "The Pursuit of Happiness"; Psychology Today; January, 2009; www.psychologytoday.com

Rubin Khoddam, PhD; "What's Your Definition of Happiness"; Psychology Today; June, 2015; wwwpsychologytoday.com

"Happiness comes when we stop complaining about the troubles we have and offer thanks for all the troubles we don't have."

~Unknown

CHAPTER TEN

THE PURSUIT OF HAPP(Y)NESS IS YOU

By Beth Lydia RANCHEZ

Family is Love. Family is Happiness

My family has played a significant part in all that I am today and all that I have. I was born into a poor family, the eldest of five children. My mum and dad, Jaime and Iluminada Ranchez, raised us with devotion and love, and taught us respect for ourselves and each other. They not only provided for our basic needs, but they also wanted to make sure that we had the best future they could give us. For my parents, this meant working hard so we could go to school and get a proper education. They were passionate about learning and encouraged us to always improve ourselves so we could create a future of possibilities. For that, I am so grateful, as this has taught me to excel and try my hardest in anything I do in life.

My mum and dad both came from large families and had seven siblings each. My paternal grandfather had a sugarcane plantation and my dad became a farmer just like him. Dad's inheritance from my grandparents provided my mum and dad with a home, while the land was mainly used for farming rice, corn, peanuts, mung beans, and fruit trees.

After my parents got married, they settled in a small town northeast of Luzon in the northern part of the Philippines, a farming and agricultural region. The scenery was majestic and picturesque. At the back of my parent's house was a rice field with greenery and mountains, and close by was the largest river in the Philippines, the Cagayan River. I have such fond childhood memories of swimming, gathering shellfish from the river, daydreaming of my future, and listening to my parents' storytelling.

We lived a happy, uncomplicated and humble life. My parents made sure that we were never complacent and were always grateful for the good fortune we had. Every day I am still thankful for these simple but most important lessons in life, as ultimately this wisdom is what creates a happy and fulfilled life. Although my dad probably would not have put it this way, he practiced the Law of Attraction; he always shared his blessings with others. He was generous and welcoming to strangers and vagabonds. He hosted stranded families and business people by offering them a place to stay.

My parents changed many people's lives without ever expecting anything in return or even thinking about their actions. My mom and dad believed that what makes this world a better place is our charity and compassion towards others, not material possessions. Dad would tell us that the things we enjoy—the things that bring happiness—cannot be taken into the next life, and what's important is how we put those things to use in this life. We must share them, because sharing, giving, respecting yourself and others, and loving unconditionally defines who we truly are and who we are meant to be. This is the only way to ultimate happiness.

To me, even though some people might have considered us

poor, my parents were the happiest and wealthiest people I knew. The way they raised us and what we have become is not measurable in monetary terms but is priceless in respect to the opportunities that their hard work, love, and dedication have created for us.

My mum and dad were never able to get university degrees. My mum was smart and very good at business. I'll never forget her excitement when we came home from school and talked about our day and what we'd learned and showed her our homework. To her, those moments were treasures, devoured like chocolates, one by one, slowly and deliberately. We have since all graduated from university and fulfilled our parents' life goal: for us to have a life of opportunity and choice. The happiness and pride that this has given my parents still fill me every day with love, hope, and happiness.

Despite the love and joy we shared, our life also had its challenges. When I was 12 years old, someone entered our home and assaulted my dad. After the attack, my family experienced some of the most significant trials of our lives. We were lucky to have the full support of our extended family who looked after my brothers and sisters while my dad was recovering in the hospital.

During these trying times, being the eldest of five children, I decided I wanted to help my parents financially. I entered the workforce at this very young and delicate age, and I went to work the land. My pay was a meager five Philippine pesos (or 15 cents USD) per day. Every day I had to walk ten kilometers just to get to the work site, but despite this, I felt good about myself. I earned real money and contributed in a small way to my family's happiness and security. I also experienced how hard it is to be a farmer. Not only was the work physically demanding, the weather conditions made it even tougher. I have learned through experience the value of money and hard work, although I do miss the freedom and peacefulness of working the land and being surrounded by the earth and its beautiful produce.

During those difficult times, I became even more inspired, motivated, and determined to work harder and to focus on my studies to pave the way for a brighter future. The farm life gave my dad a solid foundation and made me stronger and more resilient to any adversity in life. I now know that having a positive mental attitude and believing that there is always hope is the way to create the life you desire. It is your choice to be a victim or a survivor. It is your choice how you respond to events in your life and the meaning you give to it. I know that my choice is love and forgiveness over hate, and I choose happiness over sadness. Happiness really is *your choice*!

My childhood really is the foundation of my life, the resilience I have and the happiness I experience daily. Growing up amongst an abundance of fruit trees made me realize that an appreciation of nature is an essential part of my happiness. My mum's and dad's residential property was surrounded by trees. We had a big mango tree in front of our two-story house, avocado trees, papaya, and coconut trees on the left side, and at the back we had banana trees, jackfruit trees, and at least half a dozen of star apple trees.

My classmates used to visit me during weekends and enjoy the abundance of different fruits. Being able to share this abundance filled me with joy and happiness. It reinforced my belief that happiness does not come from money alone; although my parents were financially poor, we were able to share our blessings with others. These acts of kindness were repaid in so many ways, and the friendship and laughter we shared during these times will always create a huge sense of fulfillment in my life.

Providing education for us was the ultimate measure of success for my parents. Being the eldest was not always easy. I felt an enormous sense of responsibility to help my parents, as they worked so hard day in and day out without complaining, without questioning, enduring the harsh weather conditions. Rain or shine, they were in the rice field working hard to be able to send all five of us to school.

Sometimes these tough conditions made all their efforts futile. A typhoon would destroy their crops, or drought would kill all our produce. These calamities affected our income, and it was a devastating situation to observe as a child. But my beautiful parents never complained, never lost hope, and always had faith that all would be okay. They accepted the consequences, as farming mainly depends on nature's gifts. They would get back on their feet again and do whatever it took to make sure they could plant the rice again, hoping and praying for better weather conditions.

Seeing my parent's hardship, physically, financially and emotionally, gave me the courage, strength, determination, passion, and focus to study harder. And that's precisely what I did.

As much as possible, I avoided creating more problems for my parents. I used to save my allowance so that I could use the money for school contributions and other school expenses, such as buying costumes for school activities. I did anything I could to lessen their financial burden. I had my mindset focused on my studies. I was determined to finish and obtain my college degree.

With all the challenges along the way, and with determination, dedication and passion, I graduated from high school with flying colors. I topped the National College Entrance Examination (NCEE) and graduated valedictorian with gold medals and a scholarship grant to university. Because of my high NCEE results, I was automatically accepted as a scholarship student at Far Eastern University in Manila. My scholarship was an enormous financial benefit to my family.

During my first and second years in university, I was living in a ladies' dormitory, sharing a room with four other college students. I used to write down every single cent that I spent and learned the value of money and budgeting.

To cut the story short, I finished my Bachelor of Arts major in Economics and was very lucky to land a job as a researcher three weeks after my graduation. I have to say lucky, as getting a job in the Philippines is very difficult and very competitive.

I felt an enormous relief for my parents. I know I made them proud and happy to see the fruit of their hardship and suffering.

"Success is not the key to happiness. Happiness is the key to success."

– Albert Schweitzer.

When I look back at my academic life, I was so aware I had to be in charge of my own life. I loved learning, I loved my education, and I was always wanting to know more, be better, grow, and excel. My school was a public school, the only school in town, and all the children of both rich and poor families had the opportunity to get an education. I was blessed that I was surrounded by people from different backgrounds. Diversity even then was part of life, part of acceptance, part of my sense of belonging, and helped me to feel like part of a higher purpose.

During the years at school, I developed not only my academic skills but practiced and experienced compassion, a sense of responsibility towards my family and my community. I understood that if you want to change the world and make it a better place, education is the only way to make a difference. Educated people make better decisions and don't settle for second best; they live life to the fullest. My college years taught me what personal happiness is all about. It showed me that education combined with commitment, focus, and passion and the will to succeed enabled me to graduate with flying colors as the valedictorian of the class and a scholarship recipient.

During my university days, I was inspired to continue to do well and make my parents proud. It was a blessing that my scholarship eased their financial burden. I was determined, focused, and wanting to succeed in my chosen field. My mindset was to study hard and finish my degree. I firmly believe in myself and my ability to excel in whatever I do by focusing on my goals in life. My primary objective is to reach my full potential by overcoming any obstacle. I joined a few university student organizations and participated as a member of the university chapel choir. My spiritual life was as important to me as my academic life.

When I graduated with a Bachelor of Arts degree, my parents glowed with pride, and with God's grace, I landed my first job a week after graduation.

I enjoyed my first job as a researcher in a small private firm where I met many kinds of people. From there, I accepted other jobs, improving my knowledge on how to deal with people, particularly in the field of marketing. I joined the Armed Forces of the Philippines as a civilian employee. It gave me pleasure, and it was an eye-opener to see how young patriots served their communities and their country. I witnessed the bravery of young, passionate soldiers who were devoted and willing to sacrifice their happiness and families for the love of their country and dedication to their chosen careers.

It was indeed a tremendous privilege to work and travel along with high-ranking military officials; and I learned a lot, improved my knowledge, and broadened my horizons. Being in the military camp working with a lot of men also helped me to develop my personality and learn how to deal with the opposite sex, as I used to be a shy, conservative, and introverted person. All these beautiful, enjoyable experiences have given me more understanding and a better outlook on life. I learned to be tolerant, patient, compassionate, and able to understand why people behave the way they do.

My lucky star led me to migrate to Australia, and I can still vividly remember how happy and blessed I felt when I stopped over for a couple of hours and landed in Melbourne on a sunny, spring morning, fascinated by people working and enjoying their daily routines. Once I got to Sydney, I felt an overwhelming excitement to see the beautiful, vibrant, amazing, and breathtaking city that I used to only see in postcards. It was an astonishing, awesome feeling which I never dreamed of, and it was indeed a dream come true. I fell in love with the city straight away and had a feeling of *deja vu*, a sense of belonging. I was happy!

With the help of a new friend, I was able to land my first Australian job as a marketing and promotions manager, which led me to other opportunities, and from this point onwards there was no looking back.

In May 2014, my cousins invited me to visit them in Hawaii. I loved Hawaii. It is a fantastic place to live. The best part was catching up with my uncles, aunties, cousins, nephews, and nieces. They were all happy to see me. They took me to all the beautiful tourist spots, like the Diamond Head, Pearl Harbour, and the famous Waikiki Beach in Honolulu. Then I flew to Maui Island where most of my extended family lives. While in Maui, I stayed with my cousin and had an incredible, unforgettable time bonding with all of my relatives before flying to California.

Unfortunately, on the third day of my holiday in California, I received the saddest news: my beloved dad passed away. I felt numbed and shocked to hear that he was gone. We did not sleep a single minute that night, and a couple of days later I went back home to attend my dad's burial in the Philippines and pay my respects to the most influencing person in my life. I can still recall my last conversation with him – always open and honest, always caring, and always happy, seeing the best in people and the world. My father was my hero, my inspiration to be the best version of myself, and all I ever wanted was to make him happy and to make him proud.

In my life, I have learned to accept what comes my way, the good and the bad, the opportunities and the challenges.

"The two most important days in your life are the day you are born and the day you find out why."

~ Mark Twain

The above quote has resonated with me since the first time I read it and has inspired me to write down the story of my life. Not because of ego or because my story is exceptional—my story could be your story—but just to express humbly a million reasons why I am so grateful for the life that I have and for the person I have become. Finding out my *why* has made me realize the greater purpose for my existence, which has resulted in discovering my ultimate happiness.

I now live and know the very reason why I was born, the reason why I am part of my family, my friends and companions, and all the people that have touched my life in one way or another and who have left footprints of love in my heart forever, all the reasons for my happiness...

My parents molded me to the best of their abilities. They taught me to be compassionate to others, to help less fortunate people, and to be the best that I can be. I am the person that I am today because of their guidance, love, and attention. I owe my happiness to them. Each morning when I wake up, I meditate, pray, and am thankful for my parents who loved and supported me unconditionally and who worked hard and sacrificed to provide us with better education for a brighter future. As Nelson Mandela says, "Education is the most powerful weapon which you can use to change the world." This is absolutely true, and I believe it with all my heart, as I am a living testimony of it. Poverty, adversities, and trials in life are not a hindrance to anyone who's trying to reach his goals and aspirations. If you have the passion, mindset, determination, patience, and belief in yourself, you can achieve absolutely anything in life, and you can be whatever you want to be. It is up to you to determine your own destiny.

I now pass on these valuable lessons to my own family and friends. Happiness is not measured by monetary or material things. It is a product of hard work, patience, and courage to conquer the unknown with passion. For me, happiness is about reaching one's potential which gives us a sense of joy, fulfillment, and lots of love that surrounds us with a beautiful, contented peace of mind.

Though we all have different lists of dreams and goals, for most of us this is at the forefront: the possibility of living a meaningful life that affects other people for the better. Happiness is a moment-to-moment choice, one that many have a hard time making. Other people will notice if you make that choice. And you will motivate them to do the same. As research indicates, this motivation has a substantial impact on your health and future happiness. I don't think happiness is so much about what you have. What you have changes; your blessings evolve. Happiness is about how you interpret what's in front of you, how proud you are of the way you live your life, how willing you are to enjoy simple pleasures, even if things aren't perfect.

Though I haven't always done this well, today I choose to focus on the good—both in the world and in myself—to feel happy right now. How will you tune in to happiness today?

"Life is only as good as you make it!"

~ Unknown

CHAPTER ELEVEN

HAPPINESS IS OVERRATED; PEACE OF MIND IS THE GOLD!

By Meredith Voigt Hartigan

I was celebrating my AA birthday, 37 years clean and sober, when I started to reminisce about my childhood. No person was instrumental in my formative years except my grandmother, Grace Voigt. She lived right behind us, catty-corner in the corner lot. Both of my grandmothers were married for 50-plus years to alcoholics. My family tree doesn't stand tall; it rolls around knocking over furniture. I learned much from these battle-hardened matriarchs.

I also learned things from my parents. From my mother: "You can't be too thin or too rich." I have carried that statement since I was a little girl. Much to my detriment. Then I was sent to boarding school in Denver where my father lived. Though I was in Denver, I never saw my father. My mother had custody of me throughout the years. Mother lived in Rocky Ford, a tiny southern town in Colorado near Pueblo, three hours away. My new stepfather had a beautiful little cabin at Grand Lake amongst the pine trees overlooking the lake, a wonderful peaceful place where I spent my summers.

Yet it was during this time that I became anorexic. I was trying to keep thin, emulating Twiggy who was the model to follow at the time. I ended up in hospital suffering acute malnutrition. They didn't call it anorexia back then. My mother said that if I wanted to date boys, I had to gain five pounds. I was sixteen at the time, young and impressionable. So I learned how to binge and purge.

I was eventually expelled from boarding school because I smoked and constantly ran away. Mother Dearest allowed me to smoke at the cabin. She died of emphysema.

I came back from a trip to New Hampshire in a drunken stupor and was marched off to detox/treatment for 28 days. The day I was released, my friends Tom and Wayne came up from Aspen and were drinking at the Hotel Jerome. I decided to rescue them but ended up drinking, too. We decided to move the party, and since, according to Tom, I was the soberest amongst the three, I was the designated driver of a brand-new T-bird. I experienced an alcoholic blackout and ran into four parked cars.

It was all over the Aspen news. I was shamed.

Needless to say, the judge was not very kind, despite my saucing up in a mini skirt, halter top, and high-heeled shoes. I figured all I had to do was admit my mistake and say I was in AA. But the judge said, "She needs to go into treatment." And my lawyer responded with, "She just got out of treatment, 28 days in Colorado Springs." Oops.

The judge took away my license and gave me a one-year DUI and 12 months of community service work. My attitude then was, not only could I not drive, but I also had to help people in the community—free of charge. I don't get paid! I felt shame.

I had been struggling to get sober, as so many alcoholics do. Me an alcoholic? But I was still so young and beautiful. Yet my life was such a mess.

Both of my parents were alcoholics, so why not me?

My mother had gotten into AA 15 years previous in 1966. I despised their drinking and decided to kill myself in a whole new way: through drugs. And when drugs became harder to get, I turned to alcohol. Even though my mother was in AA, I had no concept of what an alcoholic was. I thought it was a skid-row drunk on Larimer Street, as it was called in the late '70s. That is not my story. When I ended up in a Denver detox center in 1980 in my mid-twenties, all I could think about was: what is a nice girl like me doing in a place like this? A woman there (probably dead by now) big, fat, black eyes, covered with tattoos, seeing hallucinations. We were given sponge slippers and little blue gowns. The sad part of that was, the men couldn't keep their urine in, and so sponge slippers were not so great!

Thank God! My mother, she made me pay for treatment. Tough love was her course.

The reality was that I used alcohol to "un-feel," to turn off, to be numb to any of my emotions and the world around me. There was a study done in 2010 by a group of leading psychology experts on the topic of alcohol and drug addiction. After an exhausting two-year analysis, their final report concluded that "alcoholics and drug addicts believe that reality is optional." This is not happiness.

When I was first sober, I met Greg when a girlfriend and I were backpacking on Maui. He would visit me in Aspen, Colorado, and we talked all the time, developing a

169

long-distance relationship. On Valentine's Day, I flew to Maui for a party on his sailboat, and he met me at the airport. The party was a bunch of cocaine and a ton of booze. White-knuckling the whole damn time!

That relationship wasn't conducive to staying clean and sober. I left Greg.

A friend in AA, an artist type, took me up a four-story building in Lahaina, Maui. He got out on the top floor, the next floor, two down, and all the way to the bottom. Visually, he was trying a make a point. "You don't have to go all the way to the bottom." Women typically go down faster. The sooner you arrest the disease, the more promising the outcome. I have been sober ever since. Thank God!

At the end of that trip, I went to a spiritual retreat in the mountains of Maui. That was all in 1982. My higher power gives me what I need and then some beyond my wildest dreams—if I don't sit in the driver's seat and every morning say, "Thy will be done." That is quintessential part of letting go and letting God. Let God do the works.

You see, I wasn't a daily drinker, but when I did drink, I couldn't stop and had 12-hour blackouts. I would take vitamins and ski one hundred times a year and run three miles every day, but then there were those times when I would end up on an airplane from a blackout thinking, *Where the hell am I going?* Those were the good times.

When I started to recover, all the people I knew who were staying sober were 50-plus years old and drank every day. They were beyond their fifties, and they had hit bottom and were daily drinkers. That wasn't the effect on me. I was a binge drinker, experimented with drugs, and had long blackouts. Finally, I accepted that I had a problem with drinking.

You see, as alcoholics, we have an allergy to alcohol. It involves the body, the mind, and the soul. It took me a long time to understand the "phenomenon of craving." Lynn and I were sitting together doing the fifth step, and I said, "I don't think I am an alcoholic!" She then said, "Take the Marty Mann test." In other words, take two drinks a day for thirty days. That scared the shit out of me. I knew that wasn't my kind of drinking." This is a progressive disease. The disease kills. It's gaining strength, doing push-ups while we are sober.

Lynn was a very smart sponsor. Me being the manipulator that I was, I told her I had been on drugs, probably that I had chased it with a drink of alcohol. There was a time at the end of my drinking whereby I didn't care what I drank!

I sobered up on January 19, 1982, so I have been sober for 37 years. Can anyone here say that? That is 37.20 years, 446.52 months, 13,589 days, 326,132 hours. The AA program works.

The Aspen AA meeting where I started was at a lady's house where she had stayed sober for 13 years by just writing letters to her sponsor every week. Imagine waiting a week to read the response. AA has grown by leaps and bounds over the years, and it's now all over the world. Thank God.

My sobriety has been an amazing and wild ride. My sponsor says we all have before and after stories. Ain't that the truth! I have participated in life. All men of faith have courage. A belief in a Power greater than myself gives me the faith to remain sober one day at a time, the courage to do self-examination consistently to combat the ever-growing ego, and the integrity to be honest and genuine with myself and others.

I am continually working on myself to be the best person I can be.

In the early years I had a tremendous amount of energy; still, do. I started running. I ran until my muscles ached. I decided to run a marathon. The training was arduous. At the time I was working for an appraisal firm doing home appraisals after I finished college at Metro State. Sylvia, A friend of mine who also ran marathons, asked me, "Did you run today?" I hated to disappoint, so...I started training for the Denver Marathon—26.2 miles—that was to be held in six months. I was a runner anyway, so six miles a day was no big stretch.

God disciplined me in ways I couldn't imagine. I woke up every day before 5 a.m. before work and was running four to six miles (9.6 kilometers) per day. I did my long run on the weekends, usually Saturday. I had to apply for the AA programs: One Day at a Time and First Things First. I took one step at a time, one day at a time, and reached my goal! My friend Sylvia stuck her head in one day and asked, "Did you run today?" I cocked my head and replied, "You betcha!" I am a morning person, so that's why I chose to run then, closing my eyes at 10 p.m. I've been that way since I got sober. Running brings me happiness.

Lao Tzu from the 6th century wrote: "A journey of 1000 miles begins with the first step." He was trying to express that those great things start from humble beginnings. I was training hard. I was at peak physicality. Then I stepped off a curb and sprained my ankle savagely three days before the marathon. I went to my doctor. I knew he wouldn't let me run. I was determined. I had just trained for six solid months. So, he said to me, "Aggressive sports medicine: take two Advil every four hours until the race." So that's what I did. "Courage to change the things I can."

That Denver Marathon was riddled with snow, wind, and rain. Many pulled out. It was a bear to run. I did it in under four hours and twenty minutes. I collapsed at the end. 26.2 miles. 42.195 kilometers. Whew!

Years ago I met Kathleen S. It was when I was working at Frontier Communications. We became friends immediately. Unbeknownst to me, she had three PhDs. Throughout the years, she became my psychologist, my spiritual advisor, and my confidant. It was she who first coined the phrase, "Happiness is overrated; peace of mind is huge."

We both explored Buddhism and felt at home. Kathleen was working at Harvard as a teacher of Eastern Studies and became a strict Buddhist and meditated one hour per day. I was studying Zen Buddhism but without the zeal. I once asked my Buddhist mentor, "What is the meaning of life?" to which he replied, "Nothing." I did not like that answer. I became a Christian. At least Christians believe in a purpose-driven life.

In 2005 my faith was tested. It was discovered that I had Hepatitis C. I was 23 years sober at the time. How could this be? My doctor had not given me a blood test in eight years. I had not shown any symptoms in 25 years, but my Hep C count was through the roof and my liver was showing signs of damage. So, straight away I started treatment, a cocktail of interferon and ribavirin. This medicine made me feel 100 years old, confused, tired, sick, and totally debilitated. Yet I still had to raise my son, Hugh, who was now a teenage boy, run a full-time business (a grooming shop), attend AA meetings, and participate in life. All in all, I was in treatment for three years. The tenacity and courage came from my absolute belief in a Higher Power.

For physical exercise, my friends and I took up ballroom dancing. As I always do with everything, I threw myself into dancing, eventually doing it five nights a week and becoming very good, extremely competent as they say. To this day, I love to dance. As Dr. Wayne Dyer said, "When you dance, your purpose is not to get to a certain place on the dance floor. It's to enjoy every step on the way." For me, the secret to dancing is to dance like nobody's watching! I danced so much that I eventually invented a shoe company that still flourishes to this day.

Finally, I was handed a clean bill of health. Again, I thank God for making me able to achieve the absolute effort required.

Retirement. That's when I really fired up! They say 60 is the new 40, and for me, that's been true.

I completed 200 hours of yoga teacher training in Denver, half the required amount. Then I sold my house and car, said farewell to my son, now an extremely competent adult, and took off for Australia. This had been a long-time goal of mine.

Australia was stunning and beautiful, and the people were fine, but I kept hearing about Bali from everybody! It's so close to Australia, and I thought, *Why not?* So I made a short trip to the Island of the Gods and fell deeply in love with this tropical paradise. So, I moved there!

Let go, let God. I let God direct me, and I believe that God wanted me to experience Bali. I moved to Ubud, yoga capital of the island, and settled into a life of quiet endeavor overlooking a river in the mountains. After a couple of years,

I decided to complete my yoga teacher training and took myself off to India. Here I was, a 66-year-old woman going to Sarvaguna Yoga at Avondale Beach, Goa, India, on her own to do 300 more hours of yoga training—in five weeks—the oldest person in the class!

I had the confidence to do what was necessary. Then the transformation really began...when a caterpillar transforms into a magnificent butterfly. It was hard, I won't lie. Not only was I amongst a group of teachers, but the asanas were also grueling, and the academic study was substantial. Although peers were a lot younger, I was up to it! I had faith in my Higher Power. Low and behold, I passed! Sometimes I amaze myself.

We got up at 6 a.m. for mantras, breathing, and meditation. We had some ginger tea at break midway and then two hours of asanas. Lunch was a vegetarian meal according to the Indian tradition. After lunch, we had philosophy and anatomy. Then asanas!

"Your vision will become clear only when you can look into your own heart. Who looks outside, dreams; who looks inside, awakes."

~ Carl Jung

Exercise to me takes me into a zone – all those endorphins created. The more endorphins, the better the results. Bob Proctor said, "One either is creating, or one is disintegrating."

Happiness and contentment: they are different yet similar. They overlap at times yet are noticeably separate. Neither relies upon the other; however, one often results in both. Many things make me happy, but a real sense of contentment is my nirvana, my peace.

My partner is an extremely competent Australian surfer. A lifetime of riding great waves has sculpted both his body and his character. He achieves his greatest happiness when he's in the ocean yet lives and breathes a deep contentment thanks to a simple purpose-driven life. He, too, is a solid member of Alcoholics Anonymous, always grateful, one day at a time. He says the path to contentment is gratitude, resulting in much happiness along the way.

At 67, I have a fantastic body, according to my Australian surfer lover seven years my junior and many honest friends, finely tuned from daily yoga and a vegetarian lifestyle. I make a point of doing yoga and meditation, and I plan to do the Bali Triathlon in October, so I am swimming, biking, and swimming most days as well. I'm having fun doing my passion and reaping the benefits. Again, when I run, dance, or practice yoga, I feel happy, but my overall lifestyle blesses me with contentment I'm grateful to feel.

Today it is Nyepi in Bali, a day of silence for the entire island. It is world-famous, even catching the attention of the U.N. where the absence of 20 tonnes of carbon in one day had them speechless. No cars or motorcycles, no planes, no people outside their homes, no Wi-Fi, no cooking, no noise. No one is to turn on the lights. Nothing. An absolute day of self-reflection. It is so remarkably quiet. It seems surreal. Wonderful.

I've learned to take responsibility for my life! Val Van De Wall wrote, "When a person takes responsibility for their life and the results they are obtaining, they will cease to blame others. Blaming others causes a person to live in a prison of their own making." When I take responsibility, blame is eliminated, and I am free to grow.

Winston Churchill said, **"Responsibility is the price of greatness."**

But most importantly, I have peace of mind. I've had much happiness especially over the last ten years, but I know that Happiness is overrated; peace of mind is the gold.

"Happiness can be found even in the darkest of times. If only one remembers to turn on the light."

~ Albus Dumbledore

CHAPTER TWELVE

Seeking the Essence

by Elizabeth Boag

The real yearning of all of us is for happiness, but—let's face it—life is troublesome, to say the least. One minute you're at the peak of the mountain bathing in success; next thing you've tumbled, bumped and bruised to rock bottom. Deadlines, bills, obligations, and the constant pressure... it's fast-paced, uncertain, and at times you can feel like a lemon being squeezed in a vice, extracting every last drop until all that's left a dry, empty shell. But what if it didn't have to be like that? What if there's another way of living? What if there's one thing that can satisfy everything? And if we were to obtain that one thing, then everything else would be achieved. Is it possible? Yes, it is possible!

Our search for happiness is similar to life in general: uncertain. Even today, in the year 2019, scientists and philosophers are trying to discover what happiness actually is. Is it a chemical balance in our brains? Is it something you can purchase? Is it simply a sense of well-being? Throughout modern society, there's been an attempt to find happiness at the cost of others, but like Newton's third law says, "For every action, there is an equal and opposite reaction." By exploiting others, one incurs some debt.

Most of us find ourselves in this current fast-paced technological society with its hypnotic fancy footwork. Such an environment invites us to get more of our comforts by the help of the external world, but we are all given a bum steer, running here and there for happiness as though in a wild goose chase.

My approach to a genuine and joyful life of happiness began with something as simple as a salad sandwich. Not just any salad sandwich, one with no butter or salt on wholemeal bread, but we'll get to that later. As I would come to learn, the choices we make, even the simple ones, can change the entire course of our lives!

I grew up in an abusive family. It was a harsh world of drug addiction and violence. My father was a hard-drinking, hard-hitting Scotsman that ruled our home with an iron fist. One of my brothers, who was 12 at the time, couldn't bear being teased and bullied by our two older stepbrothers anymore. So, as terrified as he was, he somehow summoned enough courage to stand up and face them. Our dad took a disliking to his sudden act of bravery and proceeded to give him a royal beating, which sent him flying through a thick laminated glass sliding door. He was severely bruised and received deep cuts and a broken arm! Life was tough, and we all faced challenges daily.

When I was just two and a half, my father died from emphysema, most likely caused by chain-smoking, and Mum was left to raise ten children as a widow in the rough and tumble neighborhood of Campbelltown. She did her best as a single mum, but we all faced an uphill battle trying to survive life in government housing in one of the lowest socio-economic areas in Australia.

Several of my siblings took refuge in drugs, and things took a severe turn for the worse when drug addiction and mental illness overcame some of my brothers and sisters, the effects of which tormented us all. I was eight when I first saw one of my siblings inject heroin into his veins and then slump down the wall in a drug-induced mess. The problematic things I witnessed and experienced during that time, such as the psychotic episodes, drug abuse, and the revolving door of stepdads, stripped my childhood innocence away like a hurricane destroys a town—violently and without discrimination.

I received some much-needed relief from the struggles at home when one of my elder sisters met the love of her life. Understandably he would take her away from home as much as possible on romantic getaways and adventures. The best thing about that was, they would let me tag along. We would regularly escape the chaos of Campbelltown and go on wondrous beach adventures in his four-wheel drive. On many occasions, we would visit his family that lived two and a half hours away in an old fishing town called The Entrance.

Soon afterward, my mum re-married a 40-year-old bachelor who lived at The Entrance and we all moved there to his beachfront house in this beautiful surfing town. This is where my happiness began to appear by the seaside. The soothing sounds of waves crashing on the shore at night and the glorious sunrises sparkling sunrays across the vast ocean... It was such a blessing to be a pre-schooler and having an ecstatic mermaid playground for a backyard. The seaside became my personal escape.

I would awake in the mornings and peek out my bedroom window to check the surf—in particular, the north and south point breaks, the bitou bush sand dunes that we made into cubby houses, and a five-minute walk to Ocean Baths. When things were tough at home with the arguing and fighting, I would escape to the sand dunes covered in bitou bush that flourished in the harsh salty environment. I'd sit for hours in the dunes carving stones into my personalised rock people. Oh, the joy these little animated earthy creatures would give me! I'd return home for dinner, bringing my sculptures to hand out as gifts to my broken-winged siblings. This would bring me a special kind of joy. This entire process of spending time in the warm embrace of Mother Nature's arms, expressing my creative self by sculpting rock people, and seeing the look on my brothers' and sisters' faces when I handed each of them my creative sculptures... it was an internal and natural feeling of peace.

My closest brother in age and spirit also developed a deep love for the ocean. Surfing became our number-one joy apart from the campouts with our buddies in our bitou bush cubby houses and our countless snorkeling and fishing adventures. Surfing, however, was our great love. There was excitement in waxing our boards together and packing an Esky with munchies the night before and then stretching on the shore before we strapped on our legropes. The entire ritual of surfing became our therapy, giving us the opportunity to express our pain and joy through riding the waves.

My brother went on to become an Australian Pro Junior surfing champion, and because of his passion to compete, he inspired me to start joining in on the competition and fun that the local surfing fraternity offered. The experience of belonging to this surf crew developed a connection amongst us local kids like no other, and the adventures began.

I was one of the first female surfing competitors in the area. There were no female divisions in those days, so I had to compete against the boys. My brother and I had some unforgettable experiences. We would paddle out and become submerged in the ocean's soothing embrace. It was like visiting a dear friend each time we danced upon the crest of the waves. We spent many days at the beach, riding the waves and soaking up the sun. Surfing has its way of silencing the mind because it requires extreme focus. Paddling onto a crystal clear wave would force me out of my head and into my heart.

The fresh start in the seaside town was soon overshadowed again by the influence of drug abuse. My new stepfather was a serious marijuana user and also a heavy drinker. Daily, he would invite friends, including young men, over to drink and smoke at the house in front of us all. Our lounge room became a smoking and drinking den for all the local fishermen and surfers.

A few years later, my eldest brother and sister moved back into our lives, bringing with them their heroin and amphetamine addictions. Again, our lives were turned upside down and dreams of a happy life in our new home faded into the distance. The violence, intoxication, abuse, and madness became overwhelming. It was a living nightmare. My memories of this time are like scenes from a horror film. Police and ambulances were a common sight at our home. I witnessed my stepdad beating my mum many times, even smashing her head against the wall and dragging her around the house by her hair as she screamed, with her head bleeding.

Throughout the turmoil of those years, my brother and I never gave up on our dedication and connection to the ocean. It was always our escape and our saving grace.

My mum and step father's marriage became destructive and ended a few years later, and then we moved 10 minutes north to a town called Toukley. I was introduced to the beaches of Norah Head, and my brother and I joined the Norah Head Surfing Fraternity. Things became extremely tough as Mum came to terms with yet another move and marriage breakup. Sometimes our home life was so bad that my brother and I would stay at the beach together from sunrise to sunset.

I remember the effort my brother put into teaching me how to surf. The happiness we shared every time I made it out the back to the line-up or rode a wave all the way to shore, filled us both with joy. This new northern area of coastline we'd moved to helped us discover the joy and happiness that surfing and hanging out by the ocean offered.

There were times, however, when I got caught in the dramas of experimenting with intoxications and, as a result, I was forced to feel the disappointment of letting myself down. I soon realised that the ocean was there to bring out the best in me. The glistening green waters, rolling sand dunes, and sheer cliff faces of the Norah Head coastline provided the welcomed respite I needed from the difficulties I faced at home.

"You must not lose faith in humanity. Humanity is like an ocean; if a few drops of the ocean are dirty, the ocean does not become dirty."

~ Mahatma Gandhi

After my mother's third divorce, we were always apprehensive when Mum brought a man home, as we all knew she'd made some bad choices in the past. That was until she started dating Bill, a 58-year-old bachelor and local plumber. He took us all under his wing and loved and supported us as his own. He became my protector, and I instantly decided to adopt him as my father.

Bill was a good man, and he gave us stability for the first time in our lives. It wasn't easy, because we were all dealing with the after-effects of the past damage. Three of us kids remained living at home, but we were always under the constant threat of violence from some of our older siblings who were in and out of jail at the time. My sister still living with us suffered from severe mental illness and was extremely violent towards me.

Bill supported my brother and me in our surfing and would take us to all the local competitions. On one occasion, we were preparing to attend an end-of-year surfing presentation night when my sister became violent and viciously attacked me. Out of nowhere, I was punched, kicked, and thrown around the house like a rag doll. Mum came to my aid and was also beaten, suffering a broken arm from the assault. Such random acts of violence became so bad that I was in constant fear of my sister. I developed an eating disorder, and at 12 years of age, I was diagnosed with bulimia nervosa, which I feel was the direct result of the pain and anxiety my sister put me through.

Then, as if things weren't bad enough, Bill and Mum became full-time foster carers of my five-year-old nephew and two-year-old niece, because my sister and brother-in-law were completely overcome by heroin addiction. They'd been involved in several armed robberies and various criminal activities to fund their habit, all of which had landed them in jail, leaving their young children in need of care.

So, my early adolescent years were difficult, having to endure violent abuse living with a sister suffering from drug-induced mental illness and dealing with an older sister that was in and out of jail with severe addictions and traumatizing her children who were left in my mum and stepdad's care. As I look back on those days, I have come to understand that, as harsh as it was, I was given a first-class education in where not to search for happiness.

"There is no better teacher than adversity. Every defeat, every heartbreak, every loss, contains its own seed, its own lesson on how to improve your performance next time."

~ Malcolm X

At 14 years of age, I was introduced to a women's only health club by my guardian angel and sweet older sister, who had long since made the decision to distance herself from our family. That's when I first began to understand that I could take all the pain and suffering that I'd endured and channel it into something positive. I realised that the search for happiness begins with oneself. Until then, I had just been reacting to the trauma in my life, but now, for the first time, I started to use that same trauma to fuel my actions. Suddenly it felt like I'd stopped swimming upstream against the current and began to align with the natural flow. It was like a heavy pack was lifted from my slumped, insecure, and depressed shoulders.

So, I became obsessed with health and fitness. I spoke to my mum and stepdad about the option of leaving school to finish my year 10 certificate at TAFE, where I could enroll in a Fitness Leaders course at the same time. After explaining my plan, they were very supportive of the idea and agreed to fill out the necessary paperwork.

Like a keen archer focused on the target with single-pointedness, I began to study day and night. By the age of 15, I had become a fully qualified fitness instructor and started working at a women's only fitness centre. The owners of the centre loved my enthusiasm, and within six short months, I'd worked my way up the ranks to become gym manager. The health centre became my home away from home. I must admit that the sensation of motivating and helping other women reach their goals was exhilarating.

Being of service to others was so incredibly fulfilling. The opportunity to have a positive influence in someone else's life, encouraging and supporting them to reach their goals, was a very rewarding activity. Through this work, I was able to understand the joy of being disciplined and setting my mind to something and seeing it through.

At this time, my mum and stepdad bought our local general store and I began helping them out at the sandwich bar. That's where the humble salad sandwich appeared and changed the course of my life.

Self-awareness is a fundamental part of our search for happiness. We have to stop and take a close look at ourselves and begin to really understand who we are and what exactly are we searching for. At this point in my life, I had started to appreciate that structure and discipline equals freedom. My education in fitness and nutrition had helped me to develop a healthy diet and training schedule. In particular, I had become very strict about my diet, as I was still suffering from the effects of bulimia nervosa.

So, it happened that, on this day while I was helping out at the sandwich bar, a group of tanned and salty young surfers wandered in for lunch. Most of the group grabbed a can of coke and a meat pie. But one of them, a muscular, fit-looking lad with shoulder-length brown, sun-bleached hair immediately caught my eye as he headed towards me to place an order at the sandwich bar.

"What would you like?" I shyly asked.

He replied, "A salad sandwich, please, with no butter or salt on wholemeal bread."

My heart literally skipped a beat because that's exactly what I had eaten for lunch for the past two years! I don't know how long I stood there before I came to my senses and began to make the order. After preparing the sandwich that I had made for myself time and time again, I reached across the counter and handed it to him. Our eyes met, and, at that moment, I had a sense that we somehow knew each other.

"Thanks," he said, as the group strolled out of the store. I turned to my stepdad and said, "I'm gonna marry that boy." That's where I learned that, although it's useful, you should not rely on your knowledge or reasoning capacity; the heart transaction is all important.

It takes courage to follow your heart because there's no set path and sometimes you have to take a chance. As fate would have it, I've been happily married to that boy for 20 years and he's been an integral part of my search for happiness. We instantly became close friends and discovered that we had many similar interests. Together, we've shared our love of the ocean, nature, surfing, hiking, and meditating. Most importantly, we were both searching for something and had a deep feeling that there must be more to life than what we were being offered by our peers and society.

This is where I began to peel back the hard, thick layers that I had built around myself as protection against the horrors of my upbringing. One by one, I started to come out of my shell. By training hard, pushing my body and mind, I gave buckets of blood, sweat, and tears at the gym. Every rep, every grunt of muscular agony, chipped away at the coverings of insecurity, anxiety, and fear I had developed as a child, and I started to ask myself the right questions. *Why am I chasing after happiness?* And the answers would emerge: *because it's natural for all of us to search after happiness, affection, and love.*

So, why can't I find lasting satisfaction? Lasting happiness? That was a question I had pondered for many years, and through meditation, health, fitness, an intimate relationship, childbirth, and parenting, I had come to some type of understanding but was not totally satisfied.

**"Self-reflection encourages great bravery.
Rationalisation is your greatest enemy."**

~ Awa Kenzo

Regular yoga and meditation practice triggered an in-depth purification process within me. It gave rise to a mental awareness that I had not experienced before.

Six months after I met the love of my life, I became pregnant with our first child. I was young and scared, having experienced such turmoil growing up.

My partner soon put me at ease. We went to the doctors to get confirmation of the pregnancy and a first checkup. He dropped me off, and I had these sudden horrible feelings and fears that he may not return. I remember waiting out front, anxious and frightened, then seeing his smiling face return with a hand-carved timber chest full of toys and clothes for the baby. I was so happy and relieved.

Our firstborn child was a beautiful boy whose spirit gave my husband and me a connection to pure and sacred energy, and our reality began to shift rapidly. In March 1999, my partner and I were married on a beautiful headland overlooking the surfing beaches we had loved throughout our teenage years. It was a beautiful day of happy tears and the beginning of our grand adventure!

I'm saddened to say that my mum and stepdad didn't attend the wedding, as they had received death threats from my sister saying that, if they visited, she would kill me. She was so violent and disturbed that they made the difficult decision not to participate, a decision my mum regrets to this day. My husband and I were so in love that we didn't allow any adverse influence to infringe upon our special day. But imagine for a moment having to explain to everyone why my mum wasn't present at the wedding!

To the utter astonishment of our family and friends, we sold all our worldly possessions and purchased an old campervan. Together we had developed a deep longing to search for contentment. The day after our wedding, we hit the road to travel around Australia on our honeymoon with our beautiful 18-month-old son, a young family ready to embrace what life had to offer.

We discovered many things in our travels, especially stuff about ourselves. We visited remote surfing/camping spots, alternative communities, farms, and temples. It was a journey of self-discovery but, as wonderful as it was, my yearning for answers to lasting satisfaction had not yet been fulfilled. It wasn't until we came across a humble temple on Australia's east coast that I would receive the answers I had been searching for. It was there in 1999 that I met my lifelong spiritual teacher, a visiting Sadhu from India. Through his guidance, I came to understand that real happiness does not depend on the supply of physical comforts; it is within. Ultimately what I had been searching for was lasting happiness, but in the external world, it is not possible to get that.

Through my own self-analysis, I have come to understand authentically and tangibly that material happiness is fleeting and temporary by nature. If we simply look around and examine the world, we'll see that everything here is manifest, creates some by-products, deteriorates, and becomes unmanifest. But what we are all searching for is the essence of reality, that which animates and gives life to us. To seek after that thing which sustains and energises us is the most valuable search.

Here's the kicker: consciousness is the basis of everything. Think about it for a moment. When someone is lifeless, we say they are unconscious. Consciousness is actually the basis of all reality. We can also call it spirit, soul, life force, energy, etc., etc. But the underlying principle that is beneficial on our search for genuine, lasting happiness is that everything comes from consciousness. We may appreciate the outward form, the beautiful figure, style, or sound so that many things may be appreciated, but the underlying essence of all these things should be our focal point. Therefore, the road that penetrates the unstable, fleeting material covering and enters into the conscious domain is the road inward, the road of introspection.

"Your vision will become clear only when you can look into your own heart. Who looks outside, dreams; who looks inside, awakens."

~ C.G. Jung

So, this may be where I lose many readers. When one mentions the spiritual path, for many people, this immediately conjures up images of orange-clad monks, naked ash-covered sadhus, or eccentric, reclusive hippies. This is a common misconception, but spirituality is a broad term given to those who are seeking the truth. A sincere seeker of the truth is not required to retreat into a forest monastery, ashram, or cave. The nature of consciousness, or the soul, is active. Consciousness is not dead matter. It is dynamic. Therefore, spiritual life, by nature, is also vibrant, not stagnant.

After meeting my spiritual teacher and taking up the spiritual path, growth didn't suddenly slow down, and I certainly didn't become a recluse living in a remote mountain temple. My life became supercharged with dynamic energy! I became a mother to three more beautiful children and have had the most fantastic journey nourishing and guiding all four of my children into the adventurous and inquisitive young adults that they are today. I relished the wonders of nature with them when they were little, climbing trees, having picnics by the river, and collecting shells at the beach. I navigated my way through the many sleepless nights and occasional frantic trips to the hospital.

Nowadays, it's about supporting them to follow their passions and maintain a healthy work/life balance. I really appreciate the close relationship I have with my kids. We workout, surf, meditate, and organise well-being festivals together. They are such blessings in my life.

While raising four beautiful children, I enrolled in university and completed a six-year double degree in Education and Exercise/Sports Science. This was a very demanding stage of my life, working part-time to help cover the bills and years of late nights writing essays and studying for exams. Friends and co-workers would often shake their heads in disbelief at the load and intensity of what I was trying to achieve. As I would tell them even then, it's my spiritual practices that sustain me. The early morning yoga postures, the prayers, the vegetarian food, and the service are all part of a scientific process that nourishes body, mind, and spirit.

This regulated practice of connecting to the essence is not some haphazard, obscure, or sentimental imaginary exercise. It's a scientific, tangible approach, and this is what has given me the fire in the belly to push onward, providing access to a level of dedication I'd never dreamed was possible.

I also travelled extensively through India and Indonesia and worked for a year as a sports and well-being coordinator in Timor-Leste. I successfully held numerous detox and fitness retreats in Australia and Bali helping many people reclaim their well-being and awaken their life's purposes. This is just a glimpse into some of the activities I've been fortunate to be a part of. Alongside these, I continue to have my fair share of personal challenges and turmoil. The one constant throughout all these ongoing trials and tribulations has been my adherence to my spiritual practice. The internal cultivation and connection to the essence have enabled me to remain energised and balanced during all the ups and downs.

During one of my pilgrimages to India, my spiritual teacher was asked a question about the nature of love. During his response, he said the following words that resonated deeply within my heart: "Love is Sacrifice." Then he went on to give a detailed explanation, but those three words were enough to unlock a profound inner transformation and vision in the core of my heart. Suddenly, like a flash of lightning, I had a moment of pure clarity. I released the pain and suffering I had gone through in my early years. I felt compassion for my mother and father and understanding for my brothers and sisters. And I received a crystal-clear vision of my purpose: to serve with Love, Humility, Tolerance, and Respect.

This has become the essence of my inner life's purpose, to seek harmony with the environment by adjusting my angle of vision and seeing that the environment is perfect. Through this vision, no matter what adversities come my way, the journey seems to become more peaceful and everything seems to fall into place in due course of time. So, my search has arrived at the shore of service, a land of discovery where you begin to understand that service is life-giving not life-taking, and, through love and surrender, the realm of happiness will continue to unfold.

"Remember that the happiest
are not those getting more,
but those giving more."

~ H. Jackson Brown Junior

CHAPTER THIRTEEN

Journey to Happiness after Hitting the Wall

By Irene Cop

I lay on a hospital gurney spitting chunks of glass out of my mouth. Pain wracked my body, a pain so pure I felt like I was floating outside my body. The x-ray technician moved to position my leg for a different shot of my ankle, and I cried out at the excruciating knife of pain stabbing through my pelvis. Another broken bone discovered.

I had lost consciousness and driven my car right into a massive rock face in Northern Canada. And I had almost killed my two young sons in the process.

My four-year-old son, Brendon, suffered a catastrophic brain injury and was airlifted out to the nearest specialty hospital three hours away. My six-year-old son, Sean, developed post-traumatic stress disorder (PTSD) from what he had witnessed. I broke 10 bones, including my pelvis, back, and neck.

I was physically burned out and had hit the wall... literally.

The SARS epidemic of 2003 was at its height and I was under hospital quarantine. No one could visit me. Worse yet, I was going crazy with fear for my sons since I couldn't see them.

Brendon lay in an induced coma in another hospital, having undergone emergency brain surgery. It was touch and go as to whether or not he would even live. After he survived, the neurosurgeon insisted that Brendon had lost so much brain tissue that he would never again talk, walk, or use his right arm; he would be lucky to pass even the most basic level of high school.

In the meantime, Sean's life had fallen apart. In addition to the nightmares and PTSD he was suffering, his mother and best buddy had suddenly disappeared from his life. He was suspended from school due to aggression and was threatening to hurt himself. One night, Sean called me crying so hard I could barely understand him. He missed me, felt cold inside, and needed me to cuddle him. Needless to say, I was sobbing almost as hard as he was because I couldn't help him from my isolated hospital bed. Someone sent me a picture of Sean, and the sight of his vacant eyes tore me apart inside.

I was also feeling sorry for myself because of my SARS quarantine and lack of visitors. To make matters worse, it was a beautiful spring and I was the only patient on total bed rest and unable even to go outside. I noted that friends and family would only call on rainy days, and I grumpily resented them for having fun. Then I would shamefully chastise myself for expecting others to stop living just because my life was on hold.

And then...

Then there was the crushing guilt I felt over almost killing my children. I spiraled down into self-pity, fear, guilt, and depression... pouring salt on the wound of the constant physical pain.

Oh, I kept myself busy during the daytime running my clinical practice from my hospital bed. My office manager, Bruna, dropped by paperwork on a regular basis so that I could do as much as possible from my new "office." I even commandeered the second phone in the room so that I could make outgoing calls on one line and receive calls on the other. I used work to forget about everything, working away for hours. I didn't need a TV to occupy my time. For instance, I was on a business call one day when a doctor entered my hospital room. I was so in the zone, I unthinkingly apologized to my caller that I needed to hang up because someone was in my office!

Among the pain, work, and dullness, there were also moments of sheer hilarity... at least in my warped sense of humour.

Picture it. There I lay, with 10 broken bones, including both sides of my pelvis. I was only allowed to raise my bed 30 degrees. For those of you not inclined to math (like me), that was almost nothing. I might as well have been lying flat.

I was taking opioid painkillers which *totally* constipated me. I had not had a bowel movement in eight days. Yup, Eight days.

Have you ever given birth to a ten-pound baby? Now, imagine that coming out your other orifice. While lying flat on your back on top of a bedpan to catch the baby.

There I was, alone in my hospital room, gripping the side rail and sobbing from the pain, panting, "This too shall pass. This too shall pass. This too shall pass... Literally!" With that thought, I cracked myself up so that I was laughing hysterically amidst the tears.

I decided that the pain of constipation was far worse than the pain of my fractures. So, I weaned myself off of all painkillers. And since I was on blood thinners anyway, I decided to add in another one. My office manager, Bruna, brought in a care package of wine bottles and a plastic wine glass –I still have that—so that I could have a glass of wine each day with dinner. Bruna was a godsend!

In that care package were other goodies… my therapeutic devices. I couldn't receive therapy for my injuries while SARS quarantine was on, so I decided to treat myself. Every day, I would do my own rehab exercises and treat every inch of me I could reach within the bounds of my movement restrictions.

I know. Doctors make the worst patients. The staff were by turns frustrated with me, scandalized by me, laughing at me—and with me—as they came to truly like, trust, and respect me.

Progressively, many of the staff began to come to me for advice and help because those poor people were on quarantine, too. Even though they could go home at the end of each shift, they were essentially under house arrest and unable to see their own families and children. They lived with the fear that they too could contract SARS and possibly die. If they had pain, they had to suck it up because they couldn't go get therapy either. The staff and patients were definitely in it together and all felt the pain, stress, and fear of SARS.

The hospital staff did their best to take care of me and to give me relief from the prison of my room. On every fair-weather day, they would roll my bed out onto a covered balcony in the closed Occupational Therapy department so that I could spend a couple of hours outside. These moments were sheer bliss for me!

I had a new appreciation for all of the little things we tend to take for granted. Hearing the sounds of children playing on the neighbouring schoolground. Simply feeling the warm breeze against my face and breathing in the fresh air. How happy I was to just be alive!

Night times, though. The dark of night brought the swirling thoughts with no distraction to spare me from them as I lay there all alone. I was my own judge and jury, finding myself guilty as charged. I was guilty of failing as a mother, for almost killing my sons when I should have been protecting them. I was a failure as a doctor for not recognizing my own signs and symptoms of burn-out. I was a failure as a business owner because my clinic was sliding downhill without me there, increasing my financial stress.

I was so afraid that my sons would blame me and that I would lose them emotionally. After all, I hadn't been there for them when I had promised I would always protect them. I was afraid they would blame me for Brendon's injuries and for the havoc wreaked in their lives.

It truly was the bleakest time of my life.

Then, one day, I received a different type of paperwork. I received legal papers. My former husband was suing me for full custody of our children, claiming I was an incompetent mother and a danger to them.

On some level, I knew that my ex-husband was merely acting on his own terror and rage at almost losing our sons. Yet, I felt so much anger and betrayal that he would kick me while

I was down at the lowest place of my life, especially after I had worked so hard to maintain an amicable relationship following our separation two years prior.

To compound it, the fear rocketed out of control, even more than it had before. The fear that I could lose my sons physically. My inner judge and jury already agreed with my ex-husband. I was to blame. What was the use of fighting? I was overwhelmed by the emotional maelstrom ricocheting inside of me.

At that moment, I honestly wondered if I could take any more and if life was even worth living. "WHY ME?" I cried, as I wept my eyes out, all alone in my hospital room.

And yet, receiving those papers jolted me out of my emotional quicksand. I knew I had a CHOICE to either wallow in self-pity and guilt or to decide that my sons still needed me and to act.

I chose my sons.

I love my children more than anything in this world. That had always been true and became even more evident after the accident. I vowed that, from that point forward, I would look at the scars on my body and be thankful we were all alive and healthy. I knew that, even if I were to lose everything else in this world, I would have everything that was really important.

I would be happy so long as I had my sons and family.

I had always strived to be the best mother possible, and I made a further promise that I would do even better. I would play with them instead of cleaning. I would kiss and hug them even more. I would not allow outside clinical or business interests to interfere with our time together. Most importantly, I would make more time for my health so that I was in the best mental, emotional, and physical shape possible to guide my children through life.

In hindsight, I realized I had been burned out for a long time as I put everyone's needs before mine. I had to accept that I had not been taking my own advice: that you can't help anyone else until you first help yourself. I vowed that I would make my health and well-being my number one priority so that I could heal properly. I now would prioritize quality time with my children and looking after myself.

I chose to accept the fact that the accident could have happened to anyone and that the consequences could have been worse. Instead of feeling guilty, I chose to feel fortunate that we survived. I chose to be grateful for the second chance at an amazing life with my sons and family.

I also chose to show others that if it could happen to me, a doctor who should know better, it could happen to anyone. And I could show that, if my family and I could thrive after hitting the wall, so could they.

In the midst of my feelings of fear, anger, and betrayal, a glimmer of hope blossomed into joy and appreciation for having survived and for still having my sons. I also experienced an inner peace and contentment that came from knowing that we had survived against the odds for a reason. I had found an even bigger reason to live: to help others avoid burnout and the fate we'd suffered.

I knew that, far from being alone, I was just one of the millions suffering from this silent epidemic which has been encouraged by our society. We've been programmed to push ourselves to the breaking point or risk being labeled as failures or lazy.

And most people don't understand that burnout isn't just extreme fatigue or a breakdown. It can show up as brain fog, dropping the ball at home or work, making mistakes, or blowing up at coworkers or family. It might also manifest as diabetes, heart disease, or even cancer. And it can end in a car accident, possibly taking lives.

These people need someone to guide them from a feeling of drowning in overwhelm to safe footing where they can start thinking straight again. When they start to see the path, they can move rather than being frozen by anxiety.

These are people just like you and me. Really, just like me, since I was once in that place. Oh, I recognize it all too well now.

On the surface, they appear to be fine. What others don't see is the amount of time, energy, and effort it takes to keep up the appearance of "being fine." Most of the time, they're not even aware of the level of distress themselves. All they know is that they're feeling off. They can't drag themselves out of bed. It takes them twice as long to get ready for work because they're standing staring into the fridge, wondering why they opened the door. They've lost their motivation. Brain fog is permeating their minds. They're dropping the balls and feeling ashamed. They get to the end of the day and wonder where it went because they accomplished none of what they needed to get done. Secretly, they're wondering if they've lost their marbles or if they're developing early Alzheimer's. They're afraid to ask others for a second opinion or help because they're going to be put away – or laughed at.

That day in my hospital room, I had asked the Universe, "Why me?" Now, I had my answer. My children needed me to support them more than ever. I also recognized that I was uniquely qualified by my education, clinical experience, and now personal experience to attack this silent epidemic head-on and help others to heal and thrive. "Why me?" became my Why.

I could look at this accident as the ruin of my life, relationships, and finances. Instead, I decided to see it as a major reset button for my life. It gave me the opportunity to learn how to set healthy boundaries and say No. It also opened my mind to the possibility of other opportunities. I realized it was up to me to wipe the slate clean so that I could draw a new picture of what I wanted life to be like. And that started with my mindset.

I recognized that, despite the catastrophic nature of this experience, there were also positives that came out of it, and I wouldn't trade them for the world. For instance, my relationship with my father blossomed. Before the accident, we had a strained relationship in which he would act the patriarch and talk *at* me, always doling out advice on how I should live my life and what I was doing wrong—all well-intentioned.

Then I called him in that dark hour after being served with the legal papers. Poor Dad. As I sobbed incoherently into the phone, my father was at a loss for words. For perhaps the first time ever, the Problem Solver couldn't solve this problem.

Finally, my father hesitantly apologized: "I'm sorry, I don't know what I can do to make this better."

That stopped my crying short. "I know. I just needed you to listen." In that moment, our relationship changed forever.

Rather than feeling like he had to have all of the answers and solve all of the world's problems, my father seemed relieved to just *be* in our relationship. From then on, he would call me every day to ask how I was doing or to tell me a joke. Our conversations went from strained and one-sided to ones of laughter and loving support. I was so delighted to have a real relationship with my father!

Moments like these lent me the support and strength to stay positive and move forward. As soon as the SARS quarantine was lifted, and I was able to sit in a wheelchair, I discharged myself against medical advice so that I could fight the most important battle of my life: proving I was a fit mother for my children. I outfitted my house with a wheelchair lift, hospital bed, and more so that I could be at home with them. My amazingly supportive family took turns coming to stay with us to take care of my sons' physical needs which I couldn't manage.

Through this difficult and challenging time there were many moments of happiness and fulfillment. One such time that had all the makings of a calamity turned into the best of times. Due to a fluke, the power grid for most of the Northeastern United States and Canada was knocked out a couple of months after our accident. It was summertime and we were experiencing a scorching heatwave. No one could cool down or cook. Because we had one of the few pools in the neighbourhood, I called everyone I knew and invited them to cook their suppers in our backyard on my little portable barbeque and to cool off in the pool. There were easily a hundred adults and children in my backyard enjoying the impromptu pool party. Better yet, I didn't have to do anything other than just enjoy the fun!

The accident also showed me what a fantastic community we lived in. The outpouring of goodwill and support was incredible. People I had barely known came forward to help in so many different ways. Like that song, *Rainy Day People*, I found true lasting friendships in our bleakest time.

Through the good and bad, it's been a long uphill battle of healing for everyone, both emotionally and physically. I especially had to fight my own lack of belief in myself, not to mention my inner judge and jury. Through it all, my WHY sustained me even in the darkest moments, and I eventually won.

Two long stressful years later, I was fully exonerated by the legal system. It cost me of all my material wealth; yet I knew I still had an abundance of love and support. And that was infinitely more valuable.

There was one more battle to fight—this one on the inside.

It was time. Time to let go of the past. To release the anger in my heart so I could fill it with love.

It was time to forgive my ex-husband and to forgive myself. To move forward with love, I had to include myself and stop punishing myself. While I knew consciously that my car accident could have happened to anyone, my inner judge and jury were still keeping up their attacks.

I knew it was time to allow happiness to fill my life again. I realized my heavy emotional load had been sucking the life energy out of me. But how to let it go once and for all?

I discovered emotional freedom technique (EFT) or Tapping. EFT was a combination of tapping on powerful acupuncture points and using positive psychology to relieve stress, anxiety, Post-traumatic Stress, pain, and more. Since I used these same powerful acupuncture points in my clinical practice, I immediately saw how EFT could work so well. I used EFT along with coaching to wade my way through the emotional pain and guilt hiding deep inside.

I also joined Growth-U, an online personal development and conditioning company. Through their programs and amazingly supportive community, I was able to grow and actually start to love myself in a way I never had before. I was so impressed with how I felt that I most emphatically told them I wanted to be on their team, even if I were only the water girl!

As I released the heavy burden of guilt, anxiety, and emotional pain, I felt myself feeling progressively lighter, more peaceful and happier. I started to truly enjoy life again. People noticed that I started singing again. My sons were happier because I had more energy and bandwidth to give them.

Fifteen years have passed since that fateful car accident. Against all odds, Brendon learned to walk, run, and talk again. He worked harder than most children his age, enduring extra therapy and tutoring five days per week after school, from kindergarten until he graduated from high school. I cried—tears of joy this time—when he was accepted into university for engineering.

Brendon is a poster boy for neuroplasticity, the ability of the brain to change and heal itself. He is an example of possibilities for what you can achieve when you believe in yourself and are willing to work for what you want. Despite his injuries, Brendon is very fulfilled in his life and recognizes that his life experiences have honed his character in a way he would not have had the opportunity to experience so young.

Sean had a tougher time in many ways because his injury wasn't visible. More so than Brendon, Sean grappled at such a young age with the meaning of life. A few months after the accident, he asked me why we had almost died.

I responded, "Well, we should have died all things considering. So perhaps the better question should be, why did we survive?"

Sean thought about the question for a moment, then responded, "Well, Mommy, you're a doctor. So maybe you survived because you are supposed to help people."

"Maybe that's true," I replied.

"And Brendon is always fun and smiling, so maybe he survived because he is supposed to make people happy," Sean commented next.

"Wow!" I thought to myself. "What deep thinking for a six-year-old!"

Sean pondered for a bit longer, then said, "And I survived... because I am supposed to be a rich inventor and write books!"

My family and I truly have become an example of the possibility of how to survive and thrive... to know that happiness is possible no matter what curveballs life throws at you.

It has been a rollercoaster ride since that dark day in my hospital room. Through it all, my *Why* sustained me throughout these challenging times. It gave me the motivation to reject the bleak prognosis set for Brendon and to know that he could achieve so much more. It sustained me emotionally through the long custody battle and my own physical rehabilitation.

And even more, it gave me an appreciation for this life experience on so many levels. It has allowed me to truly empathize with others as they suffer adversity. I am so grateful that I have been able to empower and support all who are on the slippery slope to burnout or who have hit the wall as I did. I have made it my mission to guide people who are feeling lost and overwhelmed as they transform their lives and wellbeing. I am filled with so much joy that I am making an impact and changing lives!

These people seek guidance from me because I truly understand. I've been there. I've found a way out of the quagmire. I am passionate about the power of our minds to heal ourselves and to create our lives because I was able to use my mind to transform my own life. I now use the same tools which helped me—coaching, meditation, and EFT—to help others.

More than a doctor, I'm just a real person who has gone through hell and found her way back to happiness and health. And yet, I know that if I could do it, so could others.

I have evolved from barely surviving to thriving, basking in the abundance of love from my family, friends, and those I've helped. I am so glad when people tell me how much their lives have improved as a result of working with me. My supreme passion and mission have become to help one person at a time evolve from barely surviving to thriving. I know. I've done it and I'm no one special. If I can do it, so can others.

I am so grateful for this near-death experience, the good, the bad, and the ugly, because it has given me a whole new perspective on what really matters in life. Prior to this, I sought happiness in external sources. I could only be happy if the sun was shining, life was running smoothly, and my relationships were content.

This life reset button showed me that true happiness lies within me. It comes from loving myself so much that I am willing to put myself first, to care for myself first, and to take responsibility for my own feelings and happiness.

I have learned through incredibly difficult experience that I need to love and care for myself before I can truly help others. It has been so liberating to find that the more I take care of myself, the more energy and love I have to give others.

I have forgiven myself and anyone else who taught me to push myself to an impossible standard. I have released myself from the burden of others' judgement, knowing that is their issue rather than mine.

I now love myself in all of my perfect imperfections! It is enough to do the best I can in every moment. I have released any self-judgement if my best isn't good enough for others.

I have learned that some of the darkest moments in life can provide the deepest belly laughs, allowing for the appreciation of simply being alive in every moment. I know that I'm going to be fine no matter what curveballs life throws at me.

I have learned that material goods could add to the joy of life. However, being dependent on those to provide happiness is a dead-end street.

I have learned that I wasn't truly happy before the accident because I was depending on external circumstances to bring me joy. I was chasing that elusive Hollywood fantasy of love and success, believing that if I just achieved more, then the happiness would follow.

Instead, it only led to burnout and a life-threatening accident.

The reality is that life is about happily achieving rather than achieving to be happy.

I am incurably happy now because I choose to be happy. And because it is a conscious decision, no one can take that inner peace and contentment away from me.

I am truly so fulfilled, enjoying every moment of this life journey!

"Simplicity makes me happy."

~ Alicia Keys

AUTHOR BIOGRAPHIES

John Spender

CHAPTER ONE

John Spender is a 16 time International Best Selling author, who didn't learn how to read and write at a basic level until he was ten years old. He has since traveled the world started many businesses leading him to create the best selling book series *A Journey Of Riches*; he is an Award Winning International Speaker and Movie Maker.

John was an international NLP trainer and has coached thousands of people from various backgrounds through all sorts of challenges. From the borderline homeless to very wealthy individuals, he has helped many people to get in touch with their truth to create a life on their terms.

John's search for answers to living a fulfilling life has taken him to work with Native American Indians in the Hills of San Diego, the forests of Madagascar, swimming with humpback whales in Tonga, exploring the Okavango Delta of Botswana and the Great Wall of China. He's traveled from Chile to Slovakia, Hungary to the Solomon Islands, the mountains of Italy and the streets of Mexico.

Everywhere his journey has taken him; John has discovered a hunger among people to find a new way to live, with a yearning for freedom of expression. His belief that everyone has a book in them was born.

He is now a writing coach having worked with more than a 170 authors from 34 different countries and his publishing house MotionMediaInternational has published 20 non-fiction titles to date.

He also co-wrote and produced the movie documentary *Adversity* starring Jack Canfield, Rev. Micheal Bernard Beckwith, Dr. John Demartini and many more, coming soon in 2020. Moreover, you can bet there will be the best selling book to follow!

Gabriela Delgadillo

CHAPTER TWO

Gabriela is a world-renowned Artist and International business entrepreneur. She has worked internationally with multi-million and multi-billion-dollar companies as a Consultant and Vice President. She is Founder and CEO of The Games of Enlightenment, a global company that creates transformational card and board games.

She is a success coach and motivational speaker and a former member of The National Speaker's Association. Some of her mentors have been NSA legends such as Og Mandino, Zig Ziglar, and NSA founder Cavett Roberts.

She began her journey as an artist in 2000 and was privileged to start working under Italian Renaissance Master Frank Covino. "My art is inspired by interesting, enlightening and exceptional people like the classical masters of art and literature, and the exquisite beauty of nature." Aside from being a world-renowned artist, she is also an Art Therapist who has worked in the mental health field and teaches intuitive art classes.

Peter McIntosh

CHAPTER THREE

At our age we certainly have been blessed to have this amazing opportunity to introduce Sound Healing to the world with the aid of the powerful energies in a pyramid, the awesome frequencies of the instruments and the people heal. Sometimes perhaps we are being groomed for these opportunities, so we ask all of you to listen to your heart and follow it, we are all being given a chance to effect the big change in consciousness on the planet in our own ways, so be vigilant for that opportunity.

We welcome anyone who has read this story to visit us at the Pyramids in Ubud, Bali and share their own stories, we can always learn from others.

Peter & Lynn McIntosh

Director, Pyramids of Chi

p:+62 3619000717 | m:+62 821 45007959 | e:peter@ pyramidsofchl.com | w:www.pyramidsofchi.com | a:Ubud, Bali, Indonesia

Melissa Barkell

CHAPTER FOUR

Melissa Barkell is a 2019 US IsaBody Challenge Finalist. She has released 70 pounds by using her superfood nutrition system and creating a healthy lifestyle. Melissa enjoys running, hiking, spending time in nature, and practicing yoga. She also loves spending time with her beautiful daughter, her family, and positive people who are making our world a better place. Dogs, good coffee, and meaningful conversations make her heart happy!

Through her health, personal growth, and spiritual transformation she has found her life's purpose. Melissa believes that her transformation was not just for her, but for the thousands of people, she will inspire and coach to have their transformations. Her mission is to empower women to achieve their health and wellness goals and to create financial security for themselves and their families.

Email: m_j_barkell@yahoo.com

Facebook: www.facebook.com/mjbarkell

Instagram: www.instagram.com/mjbarkell

Konstantin Doepping

CHAPTER FIVE

Born and raised in the Southwest of Germany, Konstantin learned to love nature by celebrating wine in near by France, skiing in the Alps and hiking in the local Black Forest. Later he left at the age of 20 for an even darker place: Berlin.

After studies in marketing and years in the field of public relations, he switched profession. The past personal experiences in several jobs made clear that people are suffering from frustration and a huge need for self-realization. Questions about where to start paved the way to a national initiative for education development. Its objective is to change schools into places of participation and interactive curricula.

Add to that he is a consultant for corporate culture and organizational development. Identifying himself with the "real" new work movement, together with his partners he founded the Mindful Leadership Circle, a community aiming to establish mindfulness in the corporate world.

Ritu Bali

Chapter Six

Ritu was raised in small town of Agra, India. She studied in the Convent of Jesus and Mary at "Saint Joseph's School." She did her graduation and post graduation with the English language as her major subject. Ritu established herself as a writer from her college days itself and contributed her articles and poems in various literary magazines. Ritu's passion for English drove her to do a Ph.D. on poetry and prose work of Dom Moraes, an Indo - English writer of great repute. The topic entitled " Dom Moraes: The Man and the Poet."

Ritu worked as a postgraduate teacher in English for three years from 1993 till 1996 in Govt owned publish school before getting married.

Soon after she moved to Muscat, Oman, where she enrolled herself as a part-time teacher in a distance learning course at an Indian university and simultaneously pursued her creative writing in various literary groups. She had been contributing articles and views in various newspapers and its associated weekly magazines.

Recently Ritu released her book on Poetry " Heart to Art " - Combo of poems with a theme of painting.

Last but not least she has been involved in social activities since her childhood days receiving certificates for carrying social services, raising funds for the poor, imparting free education to underprivileged students.

Heather M. Bleakman

CHAPTER SEVEN

Throughout most of her childhood, Heather lived a sheltered life within the secure realm of her parents, grandparents, aunts, uncles and cousins. She would see these years as her golden years. Then in her pre-teens, three generations of childhood sexual abuse were exposed and challenged her family to its core.

Early childhood nightmares resurfaced and began to put a dim filter on how she saw the world and challenged her faith in mankind. Over the next decade, trauma and tragedy became the norm, and Heather used writing and dance as an outlet to speak the unspeakable, heal from the unfathomable and grieve the significant loss.

As early as ten years old, Heather entered her first writing contest, and continued to hone the craft of the "wordsmith". She published several essays locally, and began to write a collection of short stories with the dream of bringing her journey to print and share with others.

With encouragement from family, friends, high school teachers, college professors, and her spouse, she never quit writing.

Heather has faith that sharing our personal journeys is a meaningful way to connect and heal. Her story of refocusing the lens of tragedy to a lighter perspective of gratitude, self-love and forgiveness will encourage hope to the hopeless, strength to the broken and validation of value to other victims of abuse.

Sadie Konrad

CHAPTER EIGHT

Sadie Konrad was born in Sun City, CA in 1998 and has since lived in Southern California her entire life. She began mountain biking during her sophomore year of high school and has stuck with it ever since, despite all the ups and downs.

It was through this sport that Sadie realized her passion for the outdoors, and the need to get amongst it, and today she is an avid hiker and rock climber, finding much happiness in doing so with her friends and family.

New to the writing scene, Sadie is excited to be a part of this book among all the talented writers. Currently, Sadie lives with her family in Temecula, CA and has recently graduated from Mt. San Jacinto College. This fall, she will be participating in the Disney College Program in Anaheim, CA with hopes of learning more about writing and the art of storytelling.

Annette Forsythe

CHAPTER NINE

Annette Forsythe resides in Hackettstown, New Jersey with her husband of 38 years, Mark. They have four amazing daughters and are blissful about being grandparents. She loves music, reading, gardening and cooking.

Annette matriculated at the University of South Florida earning her degree in Business Administration with a minor in Psychology. She has used these skills in parenthood, her active volunteer life, and her business.

Annette is the founding partner of Netcong Physical Therapy. Expert in the world of health insurance, she is the business end of the practice, but always makes time to interact with the patients. They have been serving the area for almost twenty years.

After a lifetime of serving others, Annette has now focused on her own personal development. She is a certified growth leader, as well as a newly certified growth writer. She welcomes sharing her stories so that others may learn and see their own possibilities.

Beth Lydia RANCHEZ

Chapter Ten

Lilibeth Ranchez was born and raised in Antonio, Delfin Albano, Isabela, the northern part of the Philippines. Preferred to be called Beth.

The eldest of five kids of the late Jaime Ranchez, Senior and Iluminada Macadangdang Ranchez.

Graduated in High School as a Valedictorian with two Gold medals and a granted scholarship by the University of the Philippines but have chosen Far Eastern University where she was also awarded a full scholarship where she graduated with Bachelor of Arts major in Economics Degree Top Notcher of the National College Entrance Examination (NCEE).

Beth joined the Philippine Armed Forces in the Philippines as a Civilian employee and migrated to Australia in October of 1986. Studied Financial Planning, worked for the two big banks in Australia.

Proud mother of Cristina Ashliegh who also follows her Mum's profession in the Financial Planning Industry and Blake who is currently completing his double Degree in Computer Systems Engineer and Computer Science Engineer.

Meredith Voigt Hartigan

Chapter Eleven

Meredith Hartigan is a part of a unique group of global Certified Thinking Into Results Executive and Corporate Coaches, who locks arms with entrepreneurs, companies, organizations and individuals and helps them create and achieve the success and results they are vested in.

For the past 25 years, Meredith has worked in private industry holding various sales management positions, including owning her own companies. During these years she attended many personal growth seminars and read numerous books on this topic. Being inspired by her mentor Bob Proctor. In this program, Meredith helps her clients unlock their infinite potential and achieve the results they have always been looking for in their personal and professional lives.

The Thinking Into Results Program Coached by Meredith teaches leaders and teams how to close the gap between what they know and what they do while creating more meaningful and purpose-driven lives.

To contact Meredith for more information, please email her at denverhartigan@gmail.com.

Elizabeth Boag

CHAPTER TWELVE

Elizabeth is a follower of the Gaudiya Vaisnava spiritual lineage, in 1999 she was initiated by her Spiritual Teacher Srila Govinda Maharaj and received personal instruction in the practice of Bhakti Yoga.

Since then Elizabeth earned a Double Degree-The Bachelor of Education and Bachelor of Human Movement/Exercise Science, while concurrently raising four beautiful children and pursuing yoga training including extensive travel to India, Indonesia and Timor Leste.

Elizabeth is conversant in the life balance of optimal health and is dedicated to helping others discover the natural way to a healthy and happy lifestyle.

Irene Cop

CHAPTER THIRTEEN

Because of her own burn-out and a near-death experience, Dr. Irene is passionate about guiding overwhelmed individuals in transforming their lives and well-being 180 degrees. She focuses on using the power of the mind as she teaches tapping, meditation and other powerful tools to help people recuperate, rejuvenate, revitalize and thrive.

Dr. Irene is a Transformational Guide, Doctor, Healer and Teacher with 25 years' experience. Her educational background spans the spectrum of health and wellness. She holds both medical and chiropractic degrees, along with extensive training in acupuncture, neurology, acquired brain injury, elite coaching, stress management, lifestyle medicine, meditation, and other "brain power" techniques.

In addition to coaching and teaching, Dr. Irene is also lead author, certified coach and mastery advisor for Growth-U.

With this expansive background, Dr. Irene is uniquely positioned to successfully empower clients to take control and transform their lives through a multi-pronged approach to mind-body-spirit well-being.

AFTERWORD

I hope you enjoyed the collection of heartfelt stories, wisdom and vulnerability shared. Storytelling is the oldest form of communication, and I hope you feel inspired to take a step toward living a fulfilling life. Feel free to contact any of the authors in this book or the other books in this series.

The proceeds of this book will go to the Bali Street Kids Project, in Denpasar, Bali.

The project gives orphaned and abandoned children a home, meals and an education.

You can donate to this fantastic cause here: http://ykpa.org/

Other books in the series are…

Tapping into Courage : A Journey of Riches, Book Sixteen

https://www.amazon.com/dp/B07NDCY1KY

The Power Healing : A Journey of Riches, Book Fifteen

https://www.amazon.com/dp/B07LGRJQ2S

The Way of the Entrepreneur: A Journey Of Riches, Book Fourteen

https://www.amazon.com/dp/B07KNHYR8V

Discovering Love and Gratitude: A Journey Of Riches, Book Thirteen

https://www.amazon.com/dp/B07H23Q6D1

Transformational Change: A Journey Of Riches, Book Twelve

https://www.amazon.com/dp/B07FYHMQRS

Finding Inspiration: A Journey Of Riches, Book Eleven

https://www.amazon.com/dp/B07F1LS1ZW

Building your Life from Rock Bottom: A Journey Of Riches, Book Ten

https://www.amazon.com/dp/B07CZK155Z

Transformation Calling: A Journey Of Riches, Book Nine

https://www.amazon.com/dp/B07BWQY9FB

Letting Go and Embracing the New: A Journey Of Riches, Book Eight

https://www.amazon.com/dp/B079ZKT2C2

Making Empowering Choices: A Journey Of Riches, Book Seven

https://www.amazon.com/Making-Empowering-Choices-Journey-Riches-ebook/dp/B078JXMK5V

The Benefit of Challenge: A Journey Of Riches, Book Six

https://www.amazon.com/dp/B0778S2VBD

Personal Changes: A Journey Of Riches, Book Five

https://www.amazon.com/dp/B075WCQM4N

Dealing with Changes in Life: A Journey Of Riches, Book Four

https://www.amazon.com/dp/B0716RDKK7

Making Changes: A Journey Of Riches, Book Three

https://www.amazon.com/dp/B01MYWNI5A

The Gift In Challenge: A Journey Of Riches, Book Two

https://www.amazon.com/dp/B01GBEML4G

From Darkness into the Light: A Journey Of Riches, Book One

https://www.amazon.com/dp/B018QMPHJW

Thank you to all the authors that have shared aspects of their lives in the hope that it will inspire others to live a bigger version of themselves. I heard a great saying from Jim Rohan "You can't complain and feel grateful at the same time" at any given moment we have a chose to either feel like a victim of life or connected and grateful for it. I hope this book helps you to feel grateful and go after your dreams.